Beyond The Edge

The Search for Ultima Thule, the Northernmost Land on Earth

Beyond The Edge

The Search for Ultima Thule, the Northernmost Land on Earth

Gerald W. Johnson

Bascom Hill Publishing Group
212 3rd Avenue North, Suite 570
Minneapolis, MN 55401
612.455.2293
www.bascomhillpublishing.com

ISBN -
ISBN -
LCCN -

Book sales for North America and international:
Itasca Books, 3501 Highway 100 South, Suite 220
Minneapolis, MN 55416
Phone: 952.345.4488 (toll free 1.800.901.3480)
Fax: 952.920.0541; email to orders@itascabooks.com

Printed in the United States of America

BASCOM HILL
PUBLISHING GROUP

CONTENTS

INTRODUCTION

Five of the world's unique geographical features were first reached by explorers, adventurers, or scientists during the twentieth century: the North Pole, the South Pole, the summit of Mount Everest, the Mariana Trench, and Kaffeklubben Island.

The first three are well documented and publicized, the fourth (the world's lowest point) is adequately documented, but not widely publicized, and the fifth (the world's northernmost point of land) is neither well documented nor well publicized.

On May 13, 1900, Robert Peary and two companions reached Cape Morris Jesup on the north coast of Greenland. After making a determination of the cape's latitude, Peary believed that he had reached the world's northernmost point of land, and for nearly seven decades afterward the world accepted his claim. Then, in 1969, members of a joint American and Canadian team determined that Kaffeklubben Island, a small island some twenty miles to the east of Cape Morris Jesup was actually further north. (Robert Peary had noted the island in 1900 but didn't visit it. The island was named by the Danish explorer Lauge Koch, who observed it but also did not visit it, as he traversed the north Greenland coast in 1921.)

Since the discovery that Kaffeklubben Island was further north than Cape Morris Jesup, several smaller islands, even further north, have been seen and reached. These islands, all within several miles of Kaffeklubben Island, have proved to be transitory—emerging, existing for a few years, and then disappearing again. The first and best known of these was Oodaaq Island. Discovered in 1978, it had disappeared by 1996 when yet another island was discovered in the area. Since then several other small islands have been discovered, but, by 2004, all of these islands had seemingly disappeared also.

The transitory nature of these small islands leaves only Kaffeklubben Island to claim the distinction of the northernmost land in the world.

This unique spot has a long and varied history, which goes back some 4,000 years when the first humans traveled along the north coast of Greenland. In more recent times, its history is tied to the search for the Northwest Passage and ultimately to the goal of reaching the North Pole, both of which have overshadowed it in arctic lore. It has enticed several well-known polar explorers, but mostly as a secondary aspect of their primary objectives, and even today modern explorers attempt to fine a small bit of land to stand on and claim that they have reached Ultima Thule.

These attempts can be categorized by three periods of arctic exploration: The first period took place during the last half of the nineteenth century. It was a time when the Arctic was essentially a blank area on the world's charts. These attempts were "uncharted journeys" that took their participants into an unknown world of ice and snow.

The second period took place during the first seventy years of the twentieth century. By this time much of the Arctic had been mapped, and explorers began attempts to reach unique geographic locations: the North Pole, the northern tip of Greenland, etc. These were attempts to reach the "Ultima Thule" of ancient lore.

The third period took place during the last thirty years of the twentieth century and, in fact, continues up to the present time. Not content with the existing "farthest north" cape or island, explorers attempted, and succeeded, in finding new islands that met the criteria.

Part One: **Uncharted Journeys**

It is almost 1,000 years since Eric the Red first sighted the southern extremity of the archipelago, and from that time Norwegians, Dutch, Danes, Swedes, Englishmen, Scotchmen, and Americans have crept gradually northward up its shores until at last. . .its northern cape has been lifted out of the Arctic mists, and obscurity.

—Robert E. Peary[1]

1

Thule

Most remote of all those lands recorded.

—Pliny the Elder

In the fourth century B.C.E., the Greek explorer Pytheas of Massilia claimed to have sailed six days north of Britain until he reached a land he called "Thule." His account of the journey, *On the Ocean* or *Description of the Earth*, has been lost and so the exact location of his Thule remains a mystery. Scholars and writers have long speculated about where Pytheas may have sailed: Greenland, Iceland, Britain, or Norway? Did he actually reach any of these places, or had he just heard of a frozen northern land with six months of daylight and six months of night? In any event, he introduced into the language a word that has come to mean a remote place in the far north, a cold place beyond human habitation, a place on the edge of a frozen sea, a place not found on any map. In later times, as Europeans and Americans ventured north to unlock the mysteries of the Arctic, they were but continuing a search first undertaken by Pytheas hundreds of years earlier; a journey into unknown northern lands, a journey to a place called Thule.

Unknown to Pytheas and the Western world, another people had arrived in Thule some 2,000 years earlier. Making a long arctic journey and following a northerly route across Canada, these people had migrated across the land bridge from Asia to North America. Rather than turn south as earlier migrations had, they stayed in the arctic regions and became known to us as Eskimos. This migration eventually reached the eastern shores of Canada and then began crossing over to northwest Greenland. These people, now referred to by anthropologists as the Independence I Culture[1], are known only through what has been discovered in their archaeological record. Their story will not be a part of what follows, but it must be acknowledged that they were the first true inhabitants of Thule.

The Vikings were more than likely the first non-natives to sail up Greenland's west coast. Eric the Red reached Greenland in 985 C.E., and established a colony in the south that lasted more than 500 years. Viking artifacts found on a small island off the coast of Ellesmere Island in the upper reaches of Baffin Bay support the theory that they traveled well over a 1,000 miles up the coast.[2] Assuming these artifacts mark the northern extremity of their travels, they also mark the first in a series of *most northerly* points reached by European and American explorers in the centuries that followed.

Early in the nineteenth century, the goal of finding a Northwest Passage from the Atlantic Ocean to the Pacific Ocean was a holy grail that led both individuals and nations to venture into the frozen and uncharted north. The most famous and tragic of these early attempts to find the passage was a British expedition led by Sir John Franklin. The expedition, now known as the Franklin Expedition, was as well prepared a venture as the British Admiralty could send forth at the time. Franklin, if a bit old at 59 for the rigors of a sustained polar voyage, was nevertheless a veteran of arctic exploration. The expedition, like many early arctic ventures, may have found itself bound too closely to a military way of doing things, unable to adapt to the requirements of arctic survival.

In two ships, the *Erebus* and the *Terror*, a crew of 129 men and provisions enough for three years, the expedition sailed from England on May 19, 1845. Reaching Baffin Bay in July, they encountered two whaling ships, and after a brief exchange of greetings, the four ships parted company. The *Erebus* and the *Terror* would never be seen again.

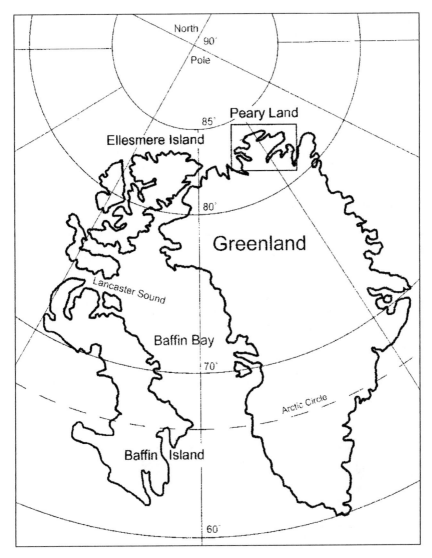

Leaving Baffin Bay, the two ships sailed west into Lancaster Sound where they spent their first winter trapped in the ice. The following spring they sailed in a southerly direction in hopes of finding an open passage to the west. After again being locked hopelessly in the ice, and following the death of Franklin in June 1847, the remaining crew members abandoned the ships and began a futile trek south. The crew's ultimate fate was first verified in 1854 when John Rae found remnants of the expedition in the Canadian tundra.

The search for Franklin and his crew lasted for 14 years and involved hundreds of people. Even today the causes of its tragic demise are not completely known, but modern science has provided some clues. Much of the expedition's food supplies were packed in tin cans sealed with molten lead. At the time, this was a relatively new and untested process. In the 1980s, a pathological examination of the bodies of three crewmen found in a Beechey Island gravesite indicated high concentrations of lead, probably caused by improper lead soldering of the cans in the sealing process. Lead poisoning would have lead to an immune deficiency, which would have decreased the body's ability to fight maladies such as scurvy and starvation.

As is often the case, advances into the unknown are paved with the graves of those who first venture there. Tragedy brings the attention of the general public to an event or a place, and this forces governments to act or at the very least it inspires adventurous individuals to act. This was true in the case of the 129 men of the Franklin Expedition. In the years following the tragedy, countless expeditions and individuals began to search the Arctic in hopes of discerning its fate. The first of these were obviously British, but it wasn't long before adventurous Americans felt compelled to join the search.

The 14-year search for Franklin was the beginning of an era of arctic exploration that would last for the next 150 years and is still going on today. The era started as a search for the Northwest Passage and ended as a continuation of the search for the elusive Thule. The early years of the era may have been British, but the later years belong mostly to Americans.

2

Cape Constitution

Beyond this cape all is surmise.

—Elisha Kent Kane[1]

In May of 1850 a privately financed expedition under the command of Edwin De Haven sailed from New York to look for Franklin and his men. The endeavor, privately funded by the wealthy New York financier Henry Grinnell, became known as the First Grinnell Expedition. De Haven had participated in the United States Exploring Expedition (the Wilkes Expedition) to Antarctica, but had no arctic experiencee.

The excursion included two ships, the *Advance* and the *Rescue,* which sailed up the west coast of Greenland, crossed Baffin Bay, headed into Lancaster Sound, and finally turned north into the Wellington channel. Here, on Beechey Island, De Haven and his surgeon were present when members of a British expedition found three graves from the Franklin Expedition. Shortly thereafter the *Advance* and the *Rescue* became locked in the ice and were not freed again until released eight months later in Baffin Bay. They then returned to the United States, having accomplished little else in their sixteen-month search.

Possibility the most important outcome of the expedition was to introduce De Haven's 30-year old surgeon, Elisha Kent Kane, to polar exploration. He became fascinated with the Arctic, and the Kane Basin, named on every map of these waters, provides a lasting memorial to his accomplishments.

After returning from the First Grinnell Expedition, he began to lobby for a second expedition, under his command. He was able to convince Henry Grinnell to again support the undertaking, and the Second Grinnell Expedition sailed north in May 1853 in the *Advance*. Ostensibly, Kane was to continue searching for clues to the fate of members of the Franklin Expedition. Was one possibility that the expedition somehow survived by reaching an open polar sea? Kane didn't really believe he would find Franklin here, but it was an excuse for him to sail north of the general search area and out into the Arctic Ocean. At this time no one knew what would be found once the Arctic Ocean was reached, but if it was an open sea, as some had speculated, Kane planned to sail the *Advance* all the way to the North Pole.

Sailing north along the west coast of Greenland, he reached the northern extent of Baffin Bay, where he entered Smith Sound. Passing through the sound, he reached a larger channel, now called the Kane Basin. Prevented by sea ice from continuing farther north, he decided to winter over. Searching for a safe place for the *Advance* to spend the winter locked in the sea ice, he found a small cove, which he named Rensselaer Harbor. The *Advance* would never leave this anchorage, and 21 months later Kane decided to abandon the ship, still locked in the ice.

Kane prepared the following explanation, which he fixed to the ship before departing:

> I regard the abandonment of the brig as inevitable. We have by actual inspection but thirty-six days' provisions, and a careful survey shows that we cannot cut more firewood without rendering our craft unseaworthy. A third winter would force us, as the only means of escaping starvation, to resort to Esquimaux habits and give up all hope of remaining by the vessel and her resources. It would in no manner advance the search after Sir John Franklin.

Under any circumstances, to remain longer would be destructive to those of our little party who have already suffered from the extreme severity of the climate and its tendencies to disease. Scurvy has enfeebled more or less every man in the expedition, and an anomalous disorder, allied to tetanus, had cost us the life of two of our most prized comrades. . . This attempt to escape by crossing the southern ice on sledges is regarded by me as an imperative duty—the only means of saving ourselves and preserving the laboriously earned results of the expedition.[2]

The story of the crew's two-and-a-half month, 500-mile journey over the ice and finally in two open boats rivals Shackleton's epic crossing of the South Atlantic half a century later.

While the Second Grinnell Expedition failed in many ways to achieve Kane's goals, it did result in the first recorded attempt to traverse the northwest coast of Greenland. In June 1854, prior to abandoning the *Advance*, Kane sent two men, William Morton and Hans Hendrick, north by dog sled along the coast of Greenland. The purpose of this trek was to push as far north as possible, both to evaluate the sea ice (was the Arctic Ocean indeed an open polar sea?) and to chart the northwest coast of Greenland.

Morton's diary records this historic journey, the first recorded attempt to traverse this section of the Greenland coast:

June 4th
I Left the vessel (the *Advance*) at 4 P.M. . . and arrived at Cache Island on the 14th.

June 18th
We set out at 0.30 A.M. . . . pursued a northerly course nearly parallel with the glacier. . . The snow was deep and free from hummocks; but, as the traveling was very heavy, we managed only about three and a half miles per hours, made our total distance but little more than twenty-six miles. . . halted at midnight to in order to take observations.

June 19th
We resume our journey at 1 A.M. During three successive hours the traveling was very heavy: the sledge would sometimes be buried in the snow, notwithstanding all our efforts to prevent it. . . The icebergs and hummocks were so close together that we could not see one hundred yards in any direction. . . We halted at 5.45 A.M. and after supper climbed

a high iceberg to select our course for the next day. . . At 10.30 P.M. we resumed our journey. . .but at the end of three miles our progress was arrested by icebergs, hummocks, and cracks. We therefore were forced to retrace our steps, and at midnight arrived at our last encampment. We then followed a westerly course, and four miles brought us to a group of icebergs, between which we found great difficulty in making our way, having to ferry ourselves occasionally over the numerous lanes of water, or to make bridges over them from the flow-pieces which were piled up in hummocks on the edges of the cracks.

June 20th
We succeeded in getting through the bergs by 2:30 A.M. We encamped at 7.20 A.M., and at 11.20 P.M. started again. . . The weather became very thick and misty. We suffered from cold, a strong N.E. wind blowing off the glacier at the time.

June 21th
At 7 A.M. we reached the mouth of a channel. . . Here stretching ahead we found open water, and before I was aware of it we had gone some distance on rotten ice, which was so weak that we could not get within a mile and a half of the open water. . . We retraced our steps carefully, calling the dogs after us, as they were very much frightened. . . and halted at 7.40 A.M.. . . After supper, or more properly breakfast, I went to the cape. . .fed the dogs, and turned in, after taking a meridian –altitude of the sun. . . We started at 11.30 P.M. One of us climbed up the ice-belt, while the other handed up the dogs and provisions, making a ladder of the sledge. It was very difficult to get around the cape, as the ice-foot was nearly all worn away, and the cliffs were very steep. . . We put the sledge on one runner, and thus passed around the most narrow part of the ice-foot. The water under us was very deep and transparent. Its temperature was 36° close alongside the ice-foot. We hear lost our thermometer.

June 22th

At 0.30 A.M. we got around the cape and found good travelling. . . The ice here is entirely broken up, and the channel is navigable for vessels of any size. . . We have traveled fifty miles to-day, and must be forty-five miles up the channel. It has been very cold, and so cloudy that I have not been able to see the sun since I entered the channel. . .

June 23th

In consequence of a gale, we did not start until 0.30 A.M. After traveling about six miles we were arrested by flow-ice in an inlet. We secured the dogs and left the sledge, as it would be impossible to transport them over these hummocks, which we succeeded in ourselves crossing with great difficulty. In this manner we traveled about four miles, and returned after sighting a high cape on the north side of a bay before us, opposite to which lay an island. On reaching the sledge we made ourselves as comfortable as possible, and resolved to go on to-morrow without it.

June 24th

We started on foot at 3 A.M., taking with us a small stock of provisions. We found great difficulty in crossing some places, where, in the absence of land–ice, we were forced to crawl over the rocks, or get on loose floating pieces of ice and jump from one to another, or else ferry ourselves until we could again reach the land.

When about nine miles on our way to-day, we saw a bear with a young one at a short distance from us. Five of our dogs had followed us, and, seeing the bear, gave chase to it.

After this delay we started, in the hope of being able to reach the cape to the north of us. Hans became tired, and I sent him more inland, where the traveling was less laborious. As I proceeded toward the cape ahead of me, the water came again close in-shore. I endeavored to reach it, but found this extremely difficult, as there were piles of broken rocks rising on the cliffs, in many places to the height of one hundred feet.

13

The cliffs above these were perpendicular, and nearly two thousand feet high. I climbed over the rubbish; but beyond it the sea was washing the foot of the cliffs, and, as there were no ledges, it was impossible for me to advance another foot. I was much disappointed, because one hour's travel would have brought me round the cape. As far as I could discern, the sea was open, a swell coming in from the northward and running crosswise, as if with a small eastern set.

June 25th
As it was impossible to get around the cape, I retraced my steps, and soon came up to Hans, who had remained a short distance behind.

After a difficult passage around the southern cape of the bay, we arrived at our camp, where we had left the sledge at 5 P.M., having been absent thirty-six hours, during which time we had traveled twenty miles due north of it.

June 26th
Before starting I took a meridian-altitude of the sun (this being the highest northern point I obtained it except one, as during the last two days the weather had been cloudy, with a gale blowing from the north,) and then set off at 4 P.M. on our return down the channel to the south.[3]

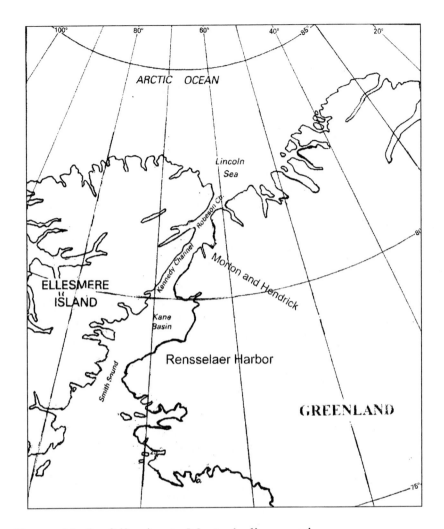

Kane adds the following to Morton's diary entries:

> The ice over the shallow bay which Morton crossed was
> hummocked, with rents through it, making very hard travel.
> He walked on over this, and saw an opening not quite eight
> miles across, separating the two islands, which I have named
> after Sir John Franklin and his comrade Captain Crozier. He
> had seen them before from the entrance of the larger bay,—
> Lafayette Bay,—but had taken them for a single island, the
> channel between them not being then in sight. As he neared
> the northern land, at the east shore which led to cape (Cape

15

Constitution,) which terminated his labors, he found only a very small ice-foot, under the lee of the headland and crushed up against the side of the rock. He went on; but the strip of land-ice broke more and more, until about a mile from the cape it terminated altogether, the waves breaking with a cross sea directly against the cape. The wind had moderated, but was still from the north, and the current ran very fast, four or five knots perhaps.

He tried to pass round the cape. It was in vain: there was no ice-foot; and, trying his best to ascent the cliffs, he could get up but a few hundred feet. Here he fastened to his walking-pole the Grinnell flag of the *Antarctic*—a well-cherished little relic, which had now followed me on two Polar voyages. This flag had been saved from the wreck of the United States sloop-of-war *Peacock*, when she stranded off the Columbia River; it had accompanied Commodore Wilkes in his far-southern discovery of an Antarctic continent. It was now its strange destiny to float over the highest northern land (81° 22′ N latitude), not only of America, but of our globe. Side by side with this were our Masonic emblems of the compass and the square. He let them fly for an hour and a half from the black cliff over the dark rock-shadowed waters, which rolled up and broke in white caps at its base.

He was bitterly disappointed that he could not get round the cape, to see whether there was any land beyond; but it was impossible. . . . .

The coast after passing the cape, he thought, must trend to the eastward, as he could at no time when below it see any land beyond.[4]

Morton's 1854 "farthest north" was the beginning of a series of historic polar expeditions that continue even to this day, some 150 years later. Individuals are still drawn to the northern edge of the world as they continue to seek *Ultima Thule*.

3

The Great Ice

A vast frozen Sahara, immeasurable to the human eye.
There was neither hill, mountain, nor gorge anywhere
in view. . . no object met the eye but our feeble tent. . .

—Isaac Israel Hayes[1]

The next person to play a role, although a minor one, in the attempts to resolve the polar enigma was Dr. Isaac I. Hayes, a man who had sailed with Kane on the Second Grinnell Expedition. Just days after completing his medical education, Hayes had signed on with Kane as his medical officer. He became fascinated with the Arctic and, after being rescued with rest of Kane's crew, he returned to the United States determined to raise funds for his own polar expedition.

Interest in the Arctic was such that he was able to secure the funding necessary to charter and outfit the schooner *United States,* and on July 9, 1860, he sailed from Boston with fourteen expedition members in addition to himself. By the beginning of September, he had reached Smith Sound where heavy ice forced him to spend the winter in a small bay 35 nautical miles southwest of Rensselaer Harbor, Kane's winter harbor. He named the harbor Port Foulke and here he went ashore and built living quarters for their winter stay.

While waiting for spring, he decided to make an exploratory journey out on to the *mer de glace* (the Greenland ice cap). His record of this journey is significant in that it gives one of the first, if not *the* first, descriptions of the interior of the Greenland ice cap.

Notwithstanding that we had no actual daylight even at noontime, yet it was light enough for traveling; the moon being full, and adding its brightness to that of the retiring sun, I felt no hesitation in carrying into execution my contemplated journey upon the glacier.

This being our first journey, of course everybody was eager to go. I had at first intended to use the dogs, with Jensen as my only companion and driver; but upon talking the matter over, I yielded to his opinion that the dogs were not available for that kind of work. Having concluded to make the journey with men, my choice fell upon (five men).

We started out on the 22nd of October. Our first camp was made at the foot of the glacier. Our next journey carried us to the top of the glacier, and it was a very serious day's business. The first attempt to scale the glacier was attended with an incident, which looked rather serious at the moment. The foremost member of the party missed his footing as he was clambering up the rude steps, and, sliding down the steep side, scattered those of who were below him to the right and left, and sent them rolling into the valley beneath. The next effort was more successful, and the end of a rope being carried over the side of the glacier, the sledge was drawn up the inclined plane, and we started off upon our journey.

On the following day we traveled thirty miles;. . .and from a surface of hard ice we had come upon an even plain of compacted snow, through which no true ice could be found after digging down to the depth of three feet. . . .The snow was covered with a crust through which the foot broke at every step, thus making the traveling very laborious.

About twenty-five miles were made during the following day, the track being of the same character as the day before; but the condition of my party warned me against the hazard of continuing the journey. The temperature had fallen to 30° below zero, and a fierce gale of wind meeting us in the face, drove us into our tent for shelter, and, after resting there for a few hours, compelled our return.

The storm steadily increased in force, and, the temperature falling lower and lower, we were all at length forced to quit the tent, and in active exercise strive to prevent ourselves from freezing.

It was not without much difficulty that the tent was taken down and bundled upon the sledge. The wind blew so fiercely that we could scarcely roll it up with our stiffened hands. The men were suffering with pain, and could only for a few moments hold on to the hardened canvas. Their fingers, freezing continually, required active pounding to keep them upon the flickering verge of life.

Our situation at this camp was as sublime as it was dangerous. We had attained an altitude of five thousand feet above the level of the sea, and we were seventy miles from the coast, in the midst of a vast frozen Sahara, immeasurable to the human eye. There was neither hill, mountain, nor gorge anywhere in view.

Our only safety was in flight; and like a ship driven before a tempest which she cannot withstand, and which threatened her ruin, we turn our backs to the gale; and hastening down the slope, we ran to save our lives.[2]

The following spring, Hayes made a short traverse up the Greenland coast to Rensselaer Harbor, the winter quarters of Kane's ill-fated ship the *Advance*. He was looking for (and expected to find) a route to the "open Polar Sea" which would allow him to sail directly to the North Pole. Deciding that such a route would not be found on the Greenland side of the Kennedy Channel, he crossed the channel and started north along the east coast of Ellesmere Island. Among his cargo was a 20-foot metal boat that was be used once he reached the "open Polar Sea." Conditions were no better here than along the Greenland coast and he soon abandoned the boat. However, he did continue north and, on May 18th, he reached a reported latitude of 81° 35′. If correct, this would be a new farthest north by land. Later investigations, however, turned up a 1° error in his reported latitude, which meant that he had not bested Morton's farthest north record.

Ice released his ship in August, and he turned her south and began the return trip to the United States. Arriving back in

Boston, Hayes found the country engaged in the Civil War and joined the Union Army, rising to the rank of colonel. After the war, he returned briefly to Baffin Island with a friend, but never again mounted a serious arctic expedition.

4

Repulse Harbor

*At midnight, last night, Captain Hall raised an American
flag on this land— The most northern site on which
any civilized flag has been planted.*

—*Captain George E. Tyson*[1]

The next polar expedition of importance was made by the most
improbable and tragic of nineteenth-century polar explorers,
Charles Francis Hall. He was a man with no training or experience
that would qualify him to lead a polar expedition. His biggest asset,
and at least initially his only asset, was his determination.

In 1859, at the age of 38, and while working as a publisher of a small
newspaper in Cincinnati, Hall became fascinated by the Arctic. This
may have been the result of the national mourning that occurred at
the death of Kane in 1857, or the popularity of Kane's two books
describing his polar adventures with the First and Second Grinnell
Expeditions. In any event, Hall became obsessed with the search
for Franklin in particular and the Arctic in general. In January1860,
leaving his wife and two-year-old son behind, he left Cincinnati for
the East Coast. There he expected to find the explorers, the men
of finance, and a ship that would enable him to pursue his dream
of becoming an arctic explorer in his own right. His determination
impressed many of the men he met, notably Henry Grinnell, the
same man who had helped finance two previous expeditions.

Hall began his new career rather modestly by securing passage on a
whaler, the *George Henry*, which sailed from New London in May
1860. His "New Franklin Research Expedition" consisted of one
person—Hall himself. Using the ship as a base as it searched for

whales, Hall managed to acquaint himself with the Arctic and its inhabitants during the two years that it sailed in the lower Canadian Archipelago. Returning to New London in September 1862, Hall was forced by the Civil War to delay his plans for a second expedition.

His newly acquired arctic experience, along with his enthusiasm, carried the day, and he was able to secure enough funding, including some from Henry Grinnell, for a modest expedition. On July 1, 1864, with a German seaman whom he hired from another whaler and two Eskimos, he sailed north as a passenger on the *Monticello*. The little group was put ashore just north of Hudson Bay. With a small boat as their only means of travel, they spent the next five years looking for clues to the fate of the Franklin Expedition. From Eskimos in the region of King William Island Hall, they were able to learn at least part of the story of the tragic demise of Franklin and his men. With this information, he sailed for home in August 1869.

After his second expedition, Hall was more determined than ever to return to the Arctic. His goal had changed, however, he now intended to push north into the "open polar sea" and sail to the Pole itself. In garnering support for this effort, he went to the top of any American explorer's list: the President of the United States. After obtaining Ulysses S. Grant's support, Congress appropriated $50,000 for a North Pole expedition in July 1870. Eight days after the bill passed the Congress, Hall received an official appointment from the White House: "You are hereby appointed to command the expedition towards the North Pole. . .signed U. S. Grant."

He immediately began to assemble a crew and to make arrangements with the Navy Department for refitting the 387-ton steam tug *Periwinkle*. This was hardly a fitting name for a ship headed to the North Pole, and Hall changed her name to the *Polaris*.

On July 3, 1871, the ship sailed from New London with roster of a 28 men, including three Eskimos. The Polaris Expedition to the North Pole was under way. After a stop in Newfoundland and several calls along the west coast of Greenland, the *Polaris* left the known world behind and sailed into Smith Sound on August 24th. The radio had yet to be invented and thus all contact with the rest of the world ended there. Three days after entering the Sound, they sailed past Rensselaer Bay, the winter quarters of Kane's ill-fated expedition. The weather and ice conditions remained favorable, and Hall continued to sail north, through what are now known as the Kennedy Channel, the Hall Basin, the Robeson Channel and finally to the Lincoln Sea on the edge of the Arctic Ocean itself. In late August, at a latitude of 82° 11′ north, the ship was finally brought to a halt by the sea ice, and immediately Hall began looking for a safe haven for the *Polaris* to spend the winter. Hall's diary did not survive the expedition, but the memoirs of George Tyson, the ship's Assistant Navigator, enlighten this part of the voyage:

Aug. 28<u>th</u>
Last night, just before midnight, at which time it was my watch, Chester came down and reported that an 'impassable barrier of ice' lay ahead of us. . .went down and reported to Captain Hall that ship could skirt around the ice by sailing a little to the south, and then steering west-north-west. At this time the sun set about 11 P.M., and rose again by 1 A.M., so that it was nearly light all the time. . . The obstructing ice which we sailed round to avoid was very thick—from ten to forty feet—. . .

We have now gained lat. 81° 35′ N. *Can't make any thing out of the charts.* As old Scoresby says," they are more a snare than a guide." But we are now at the head of Kennedy Channel, and ought soon to see *Kane's open sea*!

Today we have sailed into a bay which Morton and Hans must have mistaken for a sea, this bay to the eastward, inclining to the south. We are not deceived; we have sailed right across it. . .

Still sailing on. We have now got into a channel similar to Kennedy's, only wider, and must be part of the water mistaken for the open sea. I hope we will be able to get through, but it don't look like it now. I see some rueful countenances. I believe some of them think we are going to sail off the edge of the world, or into 'Symmes's Hole.". . . Captain Hall has called this new channel, after the Honorable Secretary of the Navy, *Robeson Channel*—a good name: without the goodwill of Secretary Robeson we should not have been here; and if the *Polaris* should get no farther, her keel has plowed through waters never parted by any ship before.

Aug. 29<u>th</u>
Went ashore in the boat with Captain Hall, and examined a bight inshore to see if it would do for a harbor. No protection; would not do. . .

Aug. 30<u>th</u>
Drifting out of Robeson Channel. . . It is blowing a gale.

Sept.2<u>nd</u>
Captain Hall requested Captain Buddington, Mr. Chester, and myself to come into the cabin; wanted to consult about attempting to proceed further north. . . *Evening.* This afternoon Captain Hall spoke to me again about our going north. He seemed to feel worried. . . But I see it's all up, and here we stop. Have ascertained that the highest latitude made by the ship was, by dead reckoning, 82° 16′; but we have drifted nearly a degree since then.

Sept. 4<u>th</u>
About 11 P.M. we had got through, and free of ice. Lowered a boat, and I went with Captain Hall ashore to examine the place for a harbor.

Sept. 5<u>th</u>
At midnight, last night, Captain Hall raised an American flag on this land—the most northern site on which any civilized flag has been planted. When it was run up, Captain Hall pronounced that he took possession "in the name of the Lord, and for the President of the United States.". . . This place, which we examined, was only a bend in the coast, and afforded no protection as a harbor. . . Captain Hall named the bight we examined "Repulse Harbor."

<u>Sept. 7th</u>

We have now brought the ship round behind an iceberg, which is aground in thirteen fathoms of water. This iceberg is about four hundred and fifty feet long, three hundred feet broad, and sixty feet high. Our latitude, by observation, 81° 38′ N., long. 61° 45′ W. . . . . We are now preparing to put permanent stores on shore, so that if the vessel gets nipped we shall have something to depend on.

Sunday. After service this morning, Captain Hall announced that he would name our winter-quarters *Thank God Harbor*, in recognition of His kind providence over us so far.

<u>Sept. 11th</u>

Commenced housing the ship with canvas, and, after the ice becomes strong enough, we shall bank her up.[2]

Less than three months later, Hall was dead, due to an acute overdose of arsenic. While Hall may have been murdered by a member of his crew, or accidentally by a self-administered dose, the exact cause will never be known. In any event, his death spelled the end of any serious attempt by the expedition to reach the pole, and it also ended further exploration that year.

The following spring and early summer ,several of the expedition members made brief attempts at further exploration. Traveling north along the coast, one party reached approximately the same latitude as the *Polaris* had the previous year. However, the captain of the ship, who was now the expedition leader, was anxious to head south as soon as the ship could be freed from the sea ice, and he therefore gave no encouragement to these attempts. Tyson's bitter disappointment with this decision is evident in his journal entry:

> Aug. 1st
> Still in Polaris Bay. What opportunities have been lost! And the expedition is to be carried back only to report a few geographic discoveries, and a few additional scientific facts. With patience we might have worked up beyond Newman Bay, and there is no telling how much further. Some one will some day reach the pole, and I envy not those who have prevented the Polaris having that chance.[3]

Most of the crew survived a harrowing retreat south from Thank God Harbor and arrived back in the United States two year later. As with Kane's expedition, the significance of what they had been able to accomplish, i.e., a new "farthest north," was lost in the repercussions of the investigation into Hall's death and the tragic loss of the *Polaris* itself.

5

Mount Hooker

I came to the conclusion it would be useless to advance any farther. . .

—Lewis A. Beaumont[1]

Following the return of the survivors of Hall's expedition, the English felt that it was time to get back in the "polar game." The British Navy outfitted two ships, the *Alert* and the *Discovery* and, under the command of Captain George S. Nares, they sailed from Portsmouth, England, in May 1875. Nares' sailing orders began thus:

> *Sir,—Her Majesty's Government having determined that an expedition of Arctic exploration and discovery should be undertaken, My Lords Commissioners of the Admiralty have been pleased to select you for the command of the said expedition, the scope and primary object of which should be to obtain the highest northern latitude, and, if possible, to reach the North Pole, and from winter quarters to explore the adjacent coasts within the reach of the traveling parties, the limits of ship navigation being confined within about the meridians of 20 and 90 West longitude.[2]*

With two ships and one-hundred-twenty men, the expedition was a major, well-funded attempt by the British to regain the initiative in arctic exploration.

The two ships reached the west coast of Greenland and then sailed north. After passing through Baffin Bay, the ships continued north through the Smith Sound, the Kane Basin, the Kennedy Channel and into the Hall Basin. The *Discovery* reached its winter quarters in Franklin Sound in late August 1875, as the *Alert* continued another sixty miles through the Robeson Channel to Cape Columbia. Here it spent the winter at a latitude of 82° 27′ N, a new "farthest north."

The following spring, several parties began a series of exploratory trips north on the sea ice and along the Greenland coast. Of particular note, with respect to all of the sledge trips from both the ships, is the fact that the sledges were hauled by men rather than dogs. Nares had no dogs, and he apparently had never even considered using them. Man-hauling the sledges added to his problems, as it did to Scott's some thirty-five years later in the Antarctic.

One of the parties, led by Albert Markam, traveled west across Ellesmere Island before turning north and traveling out on to the Arctic Ocean. They continued until they reached a latitude of 83° 20′ N, a "farthest north" that stood until bested by Peary twenty-four years later.

Another party, led by Lewis Beaumont, proceeded east across the channel and reached the Greenland coast in the vicinity of Hall's Repulse Harbor. From there they traversed in an east-northeast direction along the coast. Although not gaining much in latitude, they were the first to explore another seventy miles of the Greenland coast.

This trip was not without its struggles, as described in Beaumont's journal:

> The traveling had become worse and worse, the snow varied from two and a half to four feet in thickness, and was no longer crisp and dry, but of the consistency of moist sugar; walking was most exhausting, one literally had to climb out of the hole made by each foot in succession, the hard crust on the top, which would only just not bear you, as well as the depth of the snow preventing you from pushing forward through it, each leg sank to about three inches above the knee, and the effort of lifting them from their tight-fitting holes, soon began to tell upon the men.

> Our next march was made under a hot sun, through snow never less than three feet thick; we were parched with thirst, and obliged to halt every fifty yards to recover breath.

28

The shore for which we were making did not seem more than two miles off, so I went ahead to see if traveling was better under the cliffs. I got about a mile and-a-half ahead of the sledge in three hours, and then gave up. . . In the meantime the men had been struggling on as best they could, sometimes dragging the sledge on their hands and knees to relieve their aching legs, or hauling her ahead with a long rope and standing pulls.

The next march, May 19th, they could hardly bend their legs. . . Nobody will ever believe what hard work this becomes on the fourth day; but this may give them some idea of it. When halted for lunch, two of the men crawled for 200 yards on their hands and knees, rather than walk unnecessarily through this awful snow.

So we went on for two days, until going back seemed as hard as going on. Our provisions would compel us to start homeward on the 23rd. We could not do two miles a-day, and the men were falling sick. I did not encourage inspection of legs, and tried to make them think as little of the stiffness as possible, for I knew the unpleasant truth would soon enough be forced upon us.

I now saw to my great disappointment that we could not reach Mount Hooker, and I came to the conclusion it would be useless to advance any farther with the sledge, as turn which way we would, there was the same smooth, treacherous expanse of snow, and only two days' provisions, which would not have enabled us to reach any part of the shore; so I went back to the tent after nine and-a-half hours' hard march, and found two men unmistakably scurvy-stricken.

It seemed too cruel to have to turn back after such hard work, without reaching the land or seeing anything. But it was not to be. We left on the evening of the 22nd, a mournful and disappointed party (for the feeling was shared by all).[3]

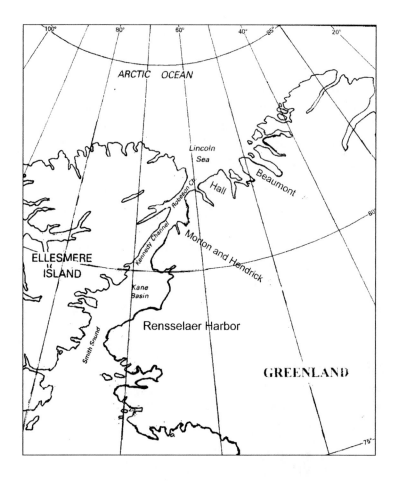

Beaumont had traveled about sixty nautical miles beyond the point where Hall had briefly landed in 1871, thus establishing a new "farthest north" on land.

Both parties, Markam's and Beaumont's, could have proceeded further were it not for the fact that scurvy had decimated most of their men. (This at a time when the cause of scurvy was known, but ways of preventing it were not always effective.) This and the fact that both parties were man-hauling their sleds severely limited the overall results of the expedition.

6

Cape Christiansen

There the national ensign was given to the breeze in the
highest latitude ever reached by man, and on land farther
north than any which had ever before met his vision.

—Adolphus W. Greely[1]

Following Nare's expedition, arctic exploration took on a new
approach; an effort by several countries to cooperate in the
scientific aspects of their polar research. Fourteen countries agreed
to coordinate meteorological observations during the International
Polar Year program, 1882-1883, by establishing a series of observation
posts around the high Arctic. In 1881, the U.S. Congress appropriated
$25,000 to fund the Lady Franklin Bay Expedition for American
participation in this program.

In command of this venture was a thirty-seven-year-old Army
Lieutenant who had never been to the Arctic, Adolphus W. Greely,
and ever since, the expedition has been referred to as the Greely
Expedition. It sailed north in July 1881, and after passing through
Baffin Bay, the Smith Sound, the Kane Basin, and the Kennedy
Channel, it arrived at Lady Franklin Bay in the northwest corner
of the Hall Basin. Here Greely established his base camp, which he
named Fort Conger. The expedition was scheduled to spend the next
two years at this remote outpost where its members were now the
world's most northerly non-native inhabitants.

The fall of 1881 was spent securing their living quarters for the long
dark winter ahead and developing sledging proficiency in anticipation
of the next year's exploration. The sun disappeared below the horizon
in the middle of October and did not appear again until the following

February. Other than daily weather records, all exploration beyond the camp came to a halt.

In March, after preliminary forays to establish advanced supply depots, two major expeditions were initiated. The first was along the Ellesmere Island coast to Cape Joseph Henry. Here open water kept it from heading north over the Arctic Ocean in an attempt to surpass the "farthest north" record of the Nare's expedition.

The second, under the command of James Lockwood, left in early April, and after traveling along the Ellesmere Island coast for a short distance crossed the channel to Greenland and proceeded northeast along the Greenland coast. By late April they had reached Beaumont's "farthest north," and Lockwood detached his support party. He, Sgt. David Brainard, and their Eskimo colleague "Fred Christiansen" then continued along the coast into the unknown.

Lockwood's official report details the following days:

May 11th
Weather still stormy, and nothing can be seen nor anything done.

At 4:10 a.m. Breakfast. Thermometer, 10°; barometer out of order. The wind, in gusts, first one side and then the other, threatened to blow down the tent.

May 12th
—At 2.45 a.m. still blowing and snowing without. Brainard and self, as well as Christiansen, suffered a great deal from cold feet, something unknown since early in April, and quite unaccountable. It interfered a great deal with our sleep, and nothing we could do seemed to help matters much in this respect. . . Some time occupied in taking an observation for latitude, the sun being dimly visible, and afterwards in filtering mercury. . . .

At 2.30 p.m. turned in; at 8.45 p.m. got up. Intended getting up at six and starting on, but we overslept ourselves. It was just as well, for the sun again disappeared, and the storm seemed to have returned as bad as ever.

<u>May 13th</u>

At 1.45 started from camp after building a small cairn near by. . . Taking a course for Pyramid Island (Brainard Island) we crossed the tide-crack without trouble, and the snow inside being generally hard, made good time. The traveling after leaving the island was very laborious through deep snow at every step. . . After this the snow got worse, till we found ourselves sinking to the thigh at every step, the dogs to the belly, and the sledge above the slots. At 11.30 a.m. reached the end of the coast-line—the traveling very bad—and continued on, turning gradually to the east till the cape, strictly speaking, was reached at 11.48 a.m. At 2 p.m. attempted observation, but gave it up—sun too obscure and weather too bad. At 5 p.m. turned in.

<u>May 14th</u>

Still blowing and snowing; no sun visible. Last night it seemed if the tent would be blown down. The rations being almost exhausted, I decided to make this cape (Cape Christiansen) my farthest and devote the little time we could stay to determining accurately my position, if the weather would allow it I feared the high cliffs here would obstruct the observations, and so moved tent, etc. about one-half mile to the west. . . En route we stopped and built a large, conspicuous cairn, about sux feet high and same in width at base. . . The weather had now cleared up beautifully, the sun bright and clear, and the atmosphere calm and mild. Most of the time from now till midnight was taken up with observations, etc.

<u>May 15th</u>

At 2.45 p.m. started with Sergeant Brainard to ascent the cliffs. . . The ascent, at first very gradual, became steeper as we went up, but we had no difficulty. . . Reached the top at 3.45 p.m. and unfurled the American flag (Mrs. Greely's) to the breeze in latitude 83° 24′ N. (according to last observation). . Left a short record in a small tin box under a few small stone (there were no larger ones), and then returned. . . At 3.50 p.m. started on return.[2]

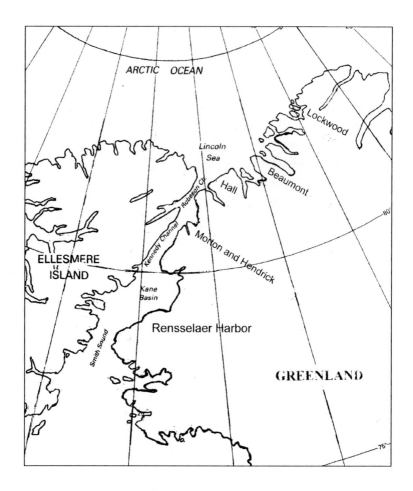

Sgt. Brainard, in his diary entry, is somewhat more expressive of their achievement:

> From observations taken along route, we are in higher latitude than ever before reached by man, and on land farther north than any was thought to exist. Once again we ran up the Stars and Stripes, this time with a feeling that warmed our spirits despite the northern breeze that swirled around us.

> . . .with rations and fuel almost vanished, we eat only every sixteen hours and then not appetizingly. Tonight—cold chocolate and frosted musk ox stew. . . We are compelled to turn back.[3]

34

Traveling along the coast and then across the Robeson Channel, they reached Fort Conger on June 1, 1882.

The promised resupply ship failed to reach Fort Conger during the summer of 1882, but other than the disappointment of no news from home, no serious problems (lack of food, etc.) were engendered by the ship's failure to reach the expedition. During the trip north in 1881 Greely's ship had not encountered any serious ice problems, either going or returning, but in 1882 the resupply ship had been unable to get any closer than two-hundred miles before being forced to turn back. Although not a disastrous outcome for Greely that year, it was a harbinger of things to come.

Again in the summer of 1883 the relief ship that was to return the party to the United States was unable to reach Lady Franklin Bay. In fact it had been caught in the ice and had gone to the bottom, thus creating a double disaster. Its crew, along with Greely's men, were now stranded in the Arctic with winter coming on.

When the relief ship failed to arrive, Greely abandoned Fort Conger and headed south in a small steam launch towing three smaller boats. It was the following June before they were rescued, and by then only seven of the original twenty-five men were still alive, and one of the seven died before the rescue ship had reached the United States.

The rescue and return of the six men aroused a great deal of interest, especially when a charge of cannibalism was made. These charges were found to be valid, but several years later it was shown to the satisfaction of most that the six survivors had not in fact been a party to the cannibalism. Fort Conger was not visited or occupied again for sixteen years until Robert Peary returned in 1899, and the "farthest north" of Lockwood, Brainard, and Christiansen was not bested until Peary passed it in 1900.

7

Independence Bay

*Have this day (July 4, 1892) reached this point, via the inland
ice from Whale Sound. We have traveled over five hundred miles.
I have named the fjord 'Independence' in honour of that day.*

—Robert E. Peary[1]

A lmost without exception, the one American name associated
with arctic exploration is Robert E. Peary. More has been written
about him than any other polar explorer, and his accomplishments are
a source of controversy even today. His claim of having reached the
North Pole in 1909 culminated eight expeditions to the Arctic over a
period of twenty-three years. Early in this period he literally claimed
the Baffin Bay-Lincoln Sea route to the pole as being exclusively his,
and he strongly dissuaded other explorers who might entertain ideas
of also using this route. Although his ultimate goal was always to be
the first to reach 90° N latitude, his attempts over the years left a rich
legacy of arctic exploration, particularly with respect to Greenland.

Peary graduated from Bowdoin College in 1877 with a degree in
civil engineering and went to work soon after in Fryeburg, Maine.
Since there were limited advancement opportunities for a young
civil engineer in the small New England town, he next took a job
with the United States Coast and Geodetic Survey in Washington,
D.C. Then, in 1881, he accepted an appointment as a civil engineer
in the United States Navy with the rank of lieutenant.

His first overseas assignment came in 1884 when he was ordered
to report for duty with the inter-oceanic canal survey in Nicaragua.
The survey lasted only three months, but during this time he earned
the praise of his commanding officer for outstanding work under

adverse conditions. More importantly he found that he had a talent for both performance and leadership under adverse conditions. After returning from Nicaragua, Peary began to rekindle his fascination for polar exploration. He had first become interested in arctic exploration when, as a boy, he read an account of Elisha Kent Kane's arctic explorations, and he now began to read all he could find on the subject. He began to see arctic exploration in general and the North Pole in particular as the way in which he intended to leave his mark on the world.

A Peary biographer elaborates:

> Peary's interest in arctic exploration actually never waned, it had lain dormant of necessity while he was in Nicaragua. Throughout his papers one sees clippings and notes on the Arctic compiled during the eighties, including the years when he was involved in the Nicaraguan project. Furthermore, Peary's interest was centered not only on arctic exploration, but also on the North Pole.[2]

Having read numerous accounts of previous arctic explorations he decided that it was time to find out firsthand just what he was going to be up against. As an arctic neophyte he knew he would be unable to secure funding for such a venture from any organization, private or governmental, and so he turned to his mother for a $500 loan to carry out his first expedition. She was not particularly happy to hear of his plans, but indulged him once again, as she had in so many ways in the past.

Considering the limited funds he put together a rather ambitious plan. His stated objectives were:

> To gain a practical knowledge of the obstacles and ice conditions of the interior of Greenland; to put to the test of actual use certain methods and details of equipment; to make such scientific observations as may be practicable; and to push into the interior as far as possible.[3]

The expedition was to involve only one person, Peary himself. He would sail north to Greenland as a paying passenger on a whaling ship and would be picked up at the end season by the same ship. Thus on June 6, 1886, he disembarked from the whaler *Eagle* at the Eskimo village of Godhavn on Disko Bay, about a third of the way up the western coast of Greenland.

His overall goal was to gain first-hand knowledge of the Greenland icecap. The "great ice" is a massive field of ice and snow, some fifteen-hundred miles in length and nine-hundred miles in width, covering most of Greenland's interior. In the center the ice is more than two miles thick. It rises from a height of a few hundred feet above sea level at the edges to a height of more than ten-thousand feet in the center, but to an observer on the surface it appears to be flat for as far as the eye can see. North, south, east or west it all appears to be the same.

In 1886 no one had any extensive experience in traveling on the icecap, let alone trying to travel across it. The Eskimos for the most part avoided it for the simple reason that there was nothing there they needed or could use. There is no animal life, and therefore it is not a source of food. It was not a convenient route to any of their destinations and, except for short trips inland from the coast, they tended to avoid any travel on it.

After reaching Godhavn, Peary traveled by boat up Disko Bay to Ritenbenk, a small village on the edge of the icecap, and it was from here he decided he would start his foray out onto the icecap. Here he also met a young Dane, Christian Maigaard, who convinced him that it would be best if he had a traveling companion with him on the ice. On July 5th, having ascended the ice cliff that marked the edge of the icecap, the two men started their journey inland, man hauling their supplies on sledges. By July 19th they had traveled about one-hundred miles inland and reached an elevation of approximately seven-hundred-fifty feet above sea level. At this point, with supplies running short, they decided it was time to turn back. Traveling on the ice itself was relatively risk free, but coming down off the ice was something else.

Peary's report of the return journey contains a harrowing account of their descent off the ice:

> The tops of all the hummocks were traversed by more or
> less numerous crevasses, and one of the crevasses, covered
> by a light snow arch, came near robbing me of my friend. We
> had pushed the catamaran across, as was our custom, till it
> rested at each end on the opposite edges of the chasm, and I
> had leaped across to pull at the same instant that Maigaard
> pushed. Unfortunately, he tripped as he sprang after, stepped
> heavily upon the snow arch, it gave way beneath him, and
> clinging to the stern of the catamaran he sank into the
> crevasse, while the bow shot into the air with a jerk that nearly
> tore it from my grasp. For a moment the sledges hung tilted
> on the lip of the chasm, with a man's life hanging on their
> quivering forms; then my weight conquered, and Maigaard's
> head came up to the surface level; the sledges crept farther
> on to the ice till the long arm of the lever was in my favour,
> and Maigaards, pale but smiling, swung himself up on the
> ice.[4]

This was the longest trip yet made by anyone onto the icecap, and
although it was not without incident, it gave Peary the confidence to
include such travel in his future plans. Some of the mysteries of the
"great ice" had begun to be unlocked, and on September 6th he was
picked up by the *Eagle* and sailed back to the United States.

The following year he again took leave from the Navy and returned
to Nicaragua in charge of the surveying work for the proposed
Nicaraguan canal route. He spent seven months there, but in the end
his work came to nothing when the Panama route was selected for
the new canal. Of particular importance to his later work was one
of the men who worked for him in Nicaragua, Matthew Henson.
Henson became invaluable to Peary and accompanied him on all of
his future arctic expeditions.

Thoughts of the Arctic were never far from Peary's mind, and
as soon as he returned from Nicaragua he began thinking about
another arctic venture. He realized that he would need more than
the $500 he obtained for his first trip, and he began thinking of ways

in which he could raise the needed money. His initial thought was to become the first man to cross the Greenland icecap, but in 1888 that dream was shattered when the Norwegian explorer Fridtjof Nansen accomplished the feat. Peary was bitterly disappointed to hear the news, but in typical fashion he set a new goal for himself: He would explore the heart of northern Greenland. At this time no one knew how far north Greenland extended. Some thought it might be as far as the North Pole itself. Nansen had crossed the narrower southern part of Greenland, but the northern two-thirds remained a geographic unknown.

In an attempt to raise the needed funds, he began soliciting various geographic societies, without luck. He then turned to lecturing both to raise money and to enhance his reputation. Finally he garnered support from the American Geographical Society, the Brooklyn Institute, and the Philadelphia Academy of Natural Sciences. This support together with contributions from several individuals, some of whom would be allowed to sail north with him, was sufficient for him to complete his plans. On June 6, 1891, Peary, with six individuals who would comprise the wintering over party and several scientists who would return with the ship sailed north on the barkentine *Kite*. His destination was Whale Sound at latitude 77° N on Greenland's western shore, much farther north than his previous expedition to Disko Bay. To the surprise and consternation of many observers, one of the six persons who would be staying over was his wife Josephine, the first non-native women to spend a winter in the Arctic.

The trip almost ended for Peary before he even reached Whale Sound. One day on board the ship he was accidentally pinned against the wheelhouse by the tiller when the rudder was suddenly struck by an ice flow. The blow broke his right leg just above the ankle, and several members of his party thought it would be prudent to turn back. Peary would have none of that, and despite being in great pain, he ordered the ship to continue on. On July 27th the *Kite* arrived at Whale Sound, where he had to be strapped to a board and carried off the ship. It took most of the autumn for him to fully recover, but in the meantime he supervised the construction of the party's living quarters. The winter was spent preparing and testing equipment that would be used for next year's traversing. Peary also spent time becoming acquainted with the Eskimos who lived in the area. From the beginning of his explorations, he recognized that success and survival depended on meeting the Arctic on its terms, and that meant knowing how the Eskimo had learned to exist in such a hostile environment.

Peary's diary records just how hostile this environment could be:

> I was awakened by the roar of the storm and the snow driving in my face. Looking over the foot of my bag, I could just see, in the faint light of day, that cutting drift had eaten off the angle of the igloo where the roof and end wall met, had completely filled that end, and was rapidly covering us. As I watched it, roof and wall melted way as fine sand before a water jet; and by the time I could arouse Dr. (Frederick A.) Cook, adjust my hood, and tighten my bag it required a good deal of effort to force myself up through the superincumbent weight of snow. The doctor also succeeded in liberating himself, but (Eivind) Astrup, who was lying on the other side of the igloo, could not get free. . . Then I crept around to the side where Astrup was, and crouching before the howling wind, tore a hole through the side wall and freed his head and body, and with the doctor's assistance, pulled him out. . . Here we were in our sleeping bags, clad only in our underclothing, and with our fur garments and footgear buried deep under the snow. . .

> We were lying out on the icecap over two thousand feet above sea level, without shelter, on the top of the drift, beneath which our snow hut was buried. . . Hear, in a sitting posture, with back to the wind and side against the drift, I sat out the night.

> . . . and learning from the doctor that he was cold. . .and as the temperature was rapidly lowering I rolled back, got the shovel, and succeeded in digging a hole, down into the snow. I then got the doctor's bag loose, pulled the sleeves out of the frozen crust, adjusted his hood, and helped him to wriggle

to the hole, into which he tumbled and curled himself up. In this way we lay for several hours, the wind gradually dying away, and the light of day increasing.

. . .and then the great yellow orb, for whose coming we had so longed, peered over the icecap south of Whale Sound. . . Neither gold, nor fame, nor aught can purchase from me the supreme memory of that moment . . . .[5]

The party then returned to their Whale Sound camp without further incident.

On May 3rd Peary began an extensive foray across the icecap. He and Astrup formed the main party, supported by three additional men (Cook, Gibson, and Henson) who would turn back. The support party turned back on May 24th as Peary and Astrup continued on in a northeasterly direction over the inland ice into the unknown. It turned out to be an exhausting trip, at times Peary and Astrup had to literally pull both the sledge and the dogs through the soft snow. After forty days they reached a high plateau that seemed to mark the northern extent of the ice cap, and possibly of Greenland.

Peary noted this historic moment:

Our silent contemplation of the sublime view at an end, I opened the box containing my transit, and set it firmly among the rocks to make my observations for position. . . The observations finished, I brought out the little silver flask of brandy which had been brought with us for use in case of sickness, and passing it to Astrup to take a thimbleful, I followed suit, and then christened the great bay spreading its white expanse before us Independence Bay, in honour of the date, July 4th. The great glacier at our right I named Academy Glacier, in honour of the Academy of Natural Sciences, Philadelphia: and the United States Navy was remembered in the name Navy Cliff, which I gave to the giant cliff on which we stood.[6]

From Navy Cliff, Independence Bay extended northwestward, and Peary assumed that it continued as a channel all the way to the west coast. There was land to the north, but he thought that this channel marked the northern extent of Greenland proper. The supposed channel, later called the "Peary Channel," was in fact a valley that appeared to be a continuation of Independence Bay when viewed from Navy Cliff. With supplies running low, he and Astrup determined that this was as far as they could safely travel and so, after building a cairn with a record of their discovery, they started for Whale Sound on July 5th. Arriving back at their camp in early August, they found

44

the *Kite* waiting to return them to the United States.

Peary had barely returned home before he began making plans for a third trip. This entailed obtaining another leave from the Navy, raising the necessary funds, securing a ship and putting together a team. Despite an exhausting lecture schedule, often delivering two lectures a day, Peary was unable to raise sufficient money for the expedition. Finally with his departure date rapidly approaching, he decided to open his ship, the *Falcon*, to visitors for a twenty-five-cent fee. Public interest in his venture was such that by this means he secured the necessary additional funds, and on July 8, 1893, he sailed north from Portland, Maine. Although this would be his third trip to Greenland, Peary called it the Second Greenland expedition.

A surprising member of the expedition again was his wife, Josephine—surprising because she was pregnant and expecting their first child in September. In addition to Peary and his wife, the expedition was composed of Henson and ten additional members. He procured sledge dogs in Labrador and Greenland and also brought along several burros, which he thought might be of use in traveling over the ice (they weren't).

On August 3rd the *Falcon* arrived in Inglefield Gulf, near his 1891-92 campsite, and here he established his new headquarters, Anniversary Lodge. He constructed a building to house the expedition members and also began hunting trips to lay-in meat for the coming winter. On August 20th the *Falcon* lifted anchor and headed back to the United States leaving Peary on his own until at least the following summer. Less than a month later, a new person was added to the expedition, Marie Ahnighito Peary. Possibly the first non-native child born in the extreme northern Arctic, she did remarkably well.

The following March, Peary began a second long journey over the Greenland icecap toward Independence Bay and the north coast. His original intent upon reaching the Navy Cliff area again was to split into three parties: one to follow the bay and continue along the northeast coast for a short distance before heading back to Anniversary Lodge across the ice, a second party would map the "Peary Channel" area, and a third party would head north on a North

Pole reconnaissance. The weather was against him this early in the season, and after traveling only one-hundred-twenty-eight miles from Anniversary Lodge, he was forced to turn back.

After resting for several weeks, Peary undertook a project of a different sort. For several years, early arctic explorers had heard stories of an "iron mountain" in the vicinity of Cape York, several days march south from Anniversary Lodge. Ascertaining that the "iron mountain" was probably a meteorite and a source of iron for the Eskimos, he convinced one of them to show him where it was. Following a perilous eleven-day journey, he arrived at the site, and after extensive digging in the snow found the "iron mountain." The Greenlanders called it "the women," and it was one of three known meteorites in the area. Without looking for the other two, Peary noted the general location and then headed back to Anniversary Lodge.

In late August, the *Falcon* returned with additional supplies and news from home. Having failed in his attempt to return to Independence Bay and unwilling to admit defeat, Peary decided not to return with the ship, but to remain another year for a second attempt. In addition to Josephine and the baby, the other members of the party were given the option of returning with the ship. It was time to "separate the men from the boys," and only two men agreed to stay. One was Henson, probably the most vital person to any success that Peary could anticipate achieving. The other was a young man, Hugh Lee, whose initial enthusiasm for coming north was the reason he was accepted as a member of the team. On August 26, 1894, the Falcon was again on its way back to the United States.

The following spring, Peary, Henson and Lee again started out again across the icecap for Independence Bay. At one-hundred-twenty-eight miles out, they expected to find the cache they had left the previous year, but after a thorough search, they had to give up and move on. This left them well short of the food they would need for the trip, but based on their previous experience they expected to find musk-oxen in the vicinity of Navy Cliff and so continued on. After several weeks they reached the cliff again, but found themselves in a rather precarious situation. As Peary noted in his book:

We were now over five hundred miles in a direct line from the lodge, and I had eleven dogs, all of them completely exhausted, and three so nearly dead that they were fit only for dog food. If we found musk-oxen down below, well and good. If we did not, not a dog in the pack, even under the most favorable circumstances and with continuous fine weather, would get more than a third of the distance back to the lodge, and the remainder of the way we must drag the sledges ourselves.[7]

They did not find any musk-oxen, but even in this tenuous situation Peary was alert to the uniqueness of what lay before them:

More than one explorer has seen the summits of a new land rise from below the sea horizon, until at last, as he stepped upon the virgin shore, they towered far above him. But never before has an explorer, after traveling for weeks in an unending day, thousands of feet above sea-level, seen the peaks and valleys of a new land lying in the yellow midnight sunlight far below him, and has literally descended from the sky upon his maiden prize.[8]

And so, without accomplishing much in the way of mapping the area, they started back. After a five-hundred-mile journey, the three starving men and their one remaining dog struggled back into camp. The trip had added very little in terms of geographic discovery, but once again Peary had demonstrated his ability to survive in the harsh polar world.

In early August, the *Kite* arrived to take them home. Disappointed by the results of his two years in the years in the Arctic, Peary was determined to salvage something from the expedition. He therefore had the *Kite* stop at Cape York on the way back, and there he loaded on board two of the meteorites he had previously located. "The women" weighed close to five-thousand-five-hundred pounds and the second, "the dog," weighed close to one-thousand pounds. The third meteorite, "the tent," weighed between ninety and one-hundred tons. Returning with the two meteorites was the only tangible success that could be claimed for the Second Greenland Expedition.

As a follow-up to the 1893-95 expedition, Peary returned briefly to Cape York during the summer of the following two years to retrieve "the tent." In 1896, ice prevented him from landing, but, in 1897, by means of some innovative engineering, he was able to load the huge meteorite onto his ship. Years later his wife sold the three meteorites to the American Museum of Natural History, where they reside today.

Part Two **Ultima Thule**

. . . and when we came within view of the next point ahead I felt that my eyes rested at last upon the Arctic Ultima Thule.

—*Robert E. Peary*[1]

Cape Morris Jesup

*It would have been a great disappointment to me, after
coming so far, to find that another's eyes had forestalled
mine in looking first upon the coveted point.*

—*Robert E. Peary[1]*

If previous expeditions had not satisfied Peary's ambitions, they had established his reputation as the premier American arctic explorer. Not long after returning from his 1893-95 expedition, and while carrying out two short polar trips in 1896 and 1897, he began planning a longer and more extensive expedition. First, he had to secure another leave of absence from the Navy. This was done when, as a political favor (not for Peary, but for a chance acquaintance of his) President McKinley issued a memorandum for a five-year leave. Next on his agenda was the matter of securing of a ship. By this time his reputation had spread well beyond the United States and, in England, a London newspaper publisher by the name of Lord Northcliffe donated a yacht, the *Windward,* in support of his arctic exploration. Peary had been hoping to obtain a ship capable of pushing north through much of the sea ice. The *Windward* with a top speed of only three and one-half knots, was hardly the answer for this requirement, but it would have to do.

More importantly, a group of New York businessmen, led by Morris K. Jesup, took an interest in Peary's work and pledged their financial support. This support was formalized when the Peary Arctic Club was formed. For the rest of Peary's expeditions, this organization was his main source of funding. The club's membership read like a Who's Who of New York's financial elite. Most of the prominent geographical features that Peary discovered in the coming years would be named after members of the club. Some support evaporated when the United States went to war with Spain after the battleship *Maine* was sunk in Havana Harbor, but enough remained for Peary to continue with his plans.

In addition to the *Windward*, he chartered a second ship, the *Hope*, to help carry his men and supplies north. The *Windward* sailed from New York on July 4, 1898, and on July 7th Peary boarded the *Hope* when it reached the Nova Scotian port of Sydney .The two ships arrived at Etah on the northwest Greenland coast in mid-August. Shortly thereafter, the *Hope* turned south and headed for home while Peary on board the *Windward* continued north to Cape D'Urville on the Canadian side of the Kane Basin.

The fall of 1898 was spent securing a supply of fresh meat for the winter, investigating unexplored areas in the region and setting out supply depots for the coming travel farther up the coast to Fort Conger, Greely's old headquarters. In January, Peary began the first of several sledge trips to Fort Conger, securing the somewhat dilapidated remains as a base for his northern exploration. The trip to Fort Conger had serious physical repercussions for Peary. After reaching the Fort and getting a fire started he noted that, "a suspicious 'wooden' feeling in the right foot led me to have my karmiks pulled off, and I found, to my annoyance, that both feet were frosted." The condition of his feet was such that it was necessary to amputate parts of seven toes, which was done under the most primitive of conditions. Six weeks later his toes were unhealed, and he could hardly stand. During the return trip to the *Windward* he was forced to ride the entire way lashed to one of the sledges, and in March he had all but the little toe of each foot amputated. A month later, before his recovery was complete, he made another round trip to Fort Conger. While there his right foot began to break down and assume an unhealthy appearance from its severe treatment. His toes would continue to bother him for the rest of his life, and thereafter he walked with a noticeable limp.

After fitting out Fort Conger as a base for the next year's northern exploration, Peary and his companions started back the two-hundred-fifty miles to Etah and the *Windward*. The rest of the 1899 summer was spent in local exploration and hunting, and in August the *Diana*, which the Peary Arctic Club had sent north, arrived with additional equipment and supplies. The two ships then spent several weeks walrus hunting in order to augment Peary's winter supplies before they headed back to the States.

In January 1900, Peary, now sufficiently recovered, started moving supplies north in anticipation of the coming season. By the end of March, with sufficient supplies in place, he began planning his northern trek. His goal was to travel out on to the Arctic sea ice in an attempt to either reach the North Pole or to establish a new "farthest north" record. He considered two possible routes: one would take him toward the pole from the north coast of Ellesmere Island, and the other would take him toward the pole from the north coast of Greenland.

He chose the latter. Given the relative late date of his start (April) and the somewhat poor condition of his dogs, he concluded that his odds of reaching the pole this year were very slim. Thus on April 11th Peary, Matthew Henson, and the Eskimo Ahngmalokto with sixteen dogs and three sledges started across the Robeson Channel toward the Greenland coast. Proceeding up the coast they passed Repulse Harbor (Hall's farthest north), Drift Point (Beaumont's farthest north), and on May 8th they reached Lockwood's cairn on Lockwood Island. Continuing on they reached Cape Washington (which can be seen from Lockwood Island), and upon rounding the cape, Peary was excited to see:

> . . .another splendid headland, with two magnificent glaciers debouching near it, rising across an intervening inlet. I knew now that Cape Washington was not the northern point of Greenland, as I had feared. It would have been a great disappointment to me, after coming so far, to find that another's eyes had forestalled mine in looking first upon that coveted northern point. . . It was evident to me now that we were very near the northern extremity of the land, and when we came within view of the next point ahead I felt that my eyes rested at last upon the Arctic Ultima Thule.[2]

53

On May 13th he reached the cape and immediately took a series of astronomic observations to determine its latitude and longitude. The results confirmed for him what he already suspected; he had indeed reached the northernmost point of the Greenland coast. Originally he called the point "North Cape," but later changed the name to "Cape Morris K. Jesup."

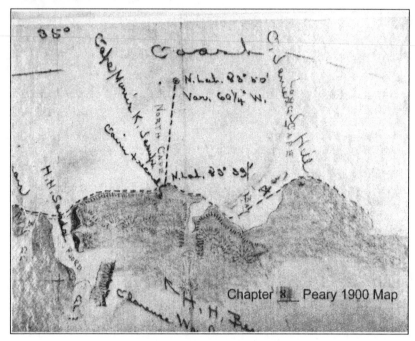

Chapter 8 Peary 1900 Map

*Many of the geographic features on his maps have two names. In lighter print would be a generic name, "Fjord," "North Cape," "Bay," etc., and then in heavier print will be a specific name, added to or replacing the generic one, "H. H. Sands Fjord," "Cape Morris K. Jesup," "Bliss Bay," etc. It is to safe to assume that these specific names, given in recognition of his financial supporters, were added later when he decided how many "friends" he had to acknowledge. Most of these names are still found on Greenland maps along with features with Danish and Inuit names.

From Cape Morris Jesup he decided to make an attempt to reach the North Pole. Given the late date he had no reasonable chance of succeeding, but he may have felt that at least an attempt was necessary to satisfy his backers. Three days of almost impossible sledging over broken ice and across huge drifts of hard snow convinced him that he would not succeed. Before starting back, however, he took the opportunity map many of the geographical features along the north Greenland coast that were visible from his offshore position.

Once back at the cape, he continued east along the coast to what today is known Cape Bridgeman (named for Herbert L. Bridgeman, another member of the Peary Arctic Club). Beyond this cape he found the coast dropping off sharply to the southeast. He continued on down the coast for two more days to Wyckoff Island (named for Clarence F. Wyckoff, another member of the club). Here, a heavy fog stopped the party for several days. After building a cairn and with supplies running short, a decision was made to abort the trek and return to Fort Conger. Peary had satisfied himself that Greenland was indeed insular (some had speculated that it might extend farther north, even as far as the pole itself) and that Cape Morris Jesup was its northernmost point.

On May 26th they again reached Cape Morris Jesup, where Peary took time to erect a prominent cairn (which still exists today), and into which he inserted the following three records:[3]

May 13, 1900—5 a.m.
Have just reached here from Etah via Ft. Conger. Left Etah March 4th Left Conger April 15th. Have with me my man Henson, and Eskimo Ahngmalokto, sixteen dogs, and three sledges; all in fair condition. Proceed to-day due north (true) over sea-ice. Fine weather. I am doing this work under the auspices of and with funds furnished by the Peary doing Arctic Club of New York City. . .

R. E. Peary
Civil Engineer, U.S. N.

May 17th
Have returned to this point. Reached 83° 50′ N. Lat. due north of here. Stopped by extremely rough ice, intersected by water cracks.

Water sky to north. Am now going east along the coast. Fine weather.

<u>May 26th</u>
Have again returned to this place. Reached point on East Coast about N. Lat. 83°. Open water all along the coast a few miles off. No land seen to north or east. Last seven days continuous fogs, wind, and snow. Is now snowing, with strong westerly wind. Temperature 20° F. Ten musk-oxen killed east of here. Expect start for Conger to-morrow.

The trip back to Fort Conger was uneventful, but Peary's recounting of the journey offers some vivid descriptions of the scenery and conditions along the way:

> . . .the north coast mountains. Very sombre and savage they looked, towering white as marble with the newly fallen snow, under their low, threatening canopy of lead-coloured clouds.
> . . The polar pack had been driven resistlessly in against the iron coast, and at every projecting point had risen to the crest of the ridge of old ice, along the outer edge of the ice-foot, in a terrific cataract of huge blocks. In places these mountains of shattered ice were one-hundred feet or more in height.[4]

Peary and his comrades arrived back at Fort Conger on June 10th. The trip had taken them two months, and there were two significant outcomes: One was to establish the northern extremes and therefore the insularity of Greenland. This established once and for all the fact that no land mass would be found at the Pole. The other outcome was that, for the next sixty-nine years, Cape Morris Jesup was accepted as the world's northernmost point of land, the world's Ultima Thule. During these years expeditions traveling along the north coast, or coming up to the cape from the south, or flying over the area all accepted it as being the northernmost point of land on the globe.*

*There is a logical explanation as to why it took so long for explorers and scientists to refute this claim. If one looks at a map of the north coast, it is seen that Cape Morris Jesup forms a natural northerly point along the coast. The land falls off both to the west and to the east. In traveling along the coast or in flying over the area the eye is naturally drawn to this phenomenon, and as one looks along the coast and sees the small island twenty miles to the east, the island appears to lie south of Cape Morris Jesup. That and the fact that well into the 60's and 70's maps of the area, relying on geographical data from explorations that dated from the early 1900's, continued to show the Cape as the world's most northerly point of land.)

The next recorded visit to the cape was in 1909. Although it didn't involve Peary himself, he was directly responsible for it. In 1906, Peary had made another failed attempt to reach the North Pole. Returning south across the Arctic Ocean the drifting sea ice carried him in an easterly direction, and he reached landfall along the north coast of Greenland about sixty miles west of Cape Morris Jesup. From here he headed west toward his ship anchored at Cape Sheridan off the coast of northwest Ellesmere Island.

In 1909 Peary again attempted to reach the North Pole. Fearing that the drifting ice might again carry him in an easterly direction as he returned, he dispatched Donald MacMillan and George Borup to set up a series of supply caches along the north Greenland coast.[5] Traveling east from the ship, the *Roosevelt,* again anchored at Cape Sheridan, they traveled east along Greenland's north coast until they reached Cape Morris Jesup where they arrived on May 7th. On May 8th a support party sent by Peary arrived with a letter from Peary to MacMillan. In part the letter read, "Arrived on board yesterday. Northern Trip entirely satisfactory. No need of Greenland depots. . . Concentrate all energies on tidal observations and line of soundings north from Morris Jesup, and use intended supplies for this purpose."

Following Peary's instructions, MacMillan headed north out over the sea ice reaching a latitude of 84° 16′ N before open water stopped him. Meanwhile Borup remained at the cape to make the tidal observations. The party began the journey back to the *Roosevelt* on

May 23rd, having spent sixteen days in the vicinity of Cape Morris Jesup.*

> *The sixteen days that MacMillan and Borup spent in the immediate vicinity of the cape are the longest time ever spent there. Other expeditions have spent more time in Peary Land but not camped at the cape.

On May 13, 1921, Lauge Koch and his Danish Bicentenary Jubilee Expedition, traveling from Fort Conger along the north coast of Greenland, also reached Cape Morris Jesup.[6] Here he examined and photographed Peary's cairn before taking a latitude observation at noon. The next day he proceeded north over the sea ice to 83° 46′ N where he took several hours of azimuth observations to visible mountain peaks for mapping purposes. After spending part of another day taking more observations, he returned south to the Cape. Here he and his companions "had an unassuming feast to mark that we had now reached the northernmost point of Greenland." Before leaving he built a small cairn at the extreme point of the cape in which he left a record along with a Danebrog (a Danish ensign).

Leaving the Cape he followed Peary's route east along the coast to Cape Bridgeman. At this point, unlike Peary who turned around and retraced his steps along the north coast, Koch returned to his headquarters by way of Independence Fjord.

Kaffeklubben Island

"Coffee Club Island"

—Lauge Koch[1]

In 1900, after leaving Cape Morris Jesup, Peary headed east along the coast and, after traveling some twenty miles, he found himself rounding another prominent cape. On his map he initially named this feature, Long Cape. Either shortly afterwards or after his return, he changed the name to Cape James J. Hill (another member of the Peary Arctic Club), the name by which the cape is still identified today.

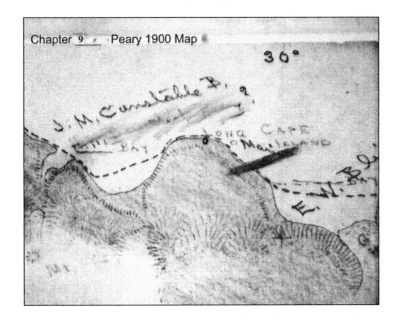

Chapter 9 — Peary 1900 Map

Just beyond the cape he sighted a small offshore island, which he added to his map and noted only with the word "Island." Later when he named other features in recognition of his financial supporters he inserted the name "Marie" prior to the word "Island." This was undoubtedly after his daughter born seven years earlier in Greenland, the first non-native child born in the high Arctic. He did nothing more with this sighting of the island, not even bothering to include it on the 1903 chart he produced for the U.S. Hydrographic Office. The logical conclusion is that he thought the island, if in fact it *was* an island, was of no geographic significance. Had he visited the island he could have claimed another arctic prize.

In 1921 Lauge Koch also continued east along the coast after stopping at Cape Morris Jesup.[2] As he passed Cape James Hill he too observed the small island just to the east of the cape and about a mile offshore. "Nothing indicates that Koch visited the island. In his report, he describes the weather on May 16-17 as bad—in the morning fog, later snow showers and a snowstorm. The snow condition for sledging that day became very bad, and the sledge dogs' conditions were described as miserable. Therefore the conclusion must be that nobody would sledge out to a small island under such conditions."[3] He did, however, give the island a name: Kaffeklubben Island, Danish for "Coffee Club" Island. The name reflected the weekly coffee club gatherings he had attended while a student in the geology department at the University of Copenhagen.

Thus the first sightings of Kaffeklubben Island were treated as relatively unimportant events both by Peary and Koch.

Current maps of the coastal area near Cape James Hill show an unnamed island to the southeast of Kaffeklubben Island, three to four times as large and just offshore from the coast. The question arises, could this be the island noted by Peary and Koch rather than Kaffeklubben Island? This seems unlikely. The ocean southwest of Kaffeklubben is very shallow and the unnamed island is not particularly prominent. A sledge traveler might not even notice it, especially in the spring when the area is covered with snow. Historically then, the first by sightings of Kaffeklubben Island took place in 1900 and 1921, first by Robert Peary and then by Lauge Koch.

The first recorded visit to the island took place on July 6, 1960, when two U.S. Army helicopters landed there. William Davies and Daniel Krinsley, geologists with the U.S. Geological Survey, were in Peary Land evaluating possible emergency aircraft landing sites for the Air Force Cambridge Research Laboratories.[4] On their way to Cape Morris Jesup, they made a stop at Kaffeklubben Island. Although not considered suitable as an aircraft-landing site, the island was of interest to the two geologists and to the Danish archaeologist, Count Eigil Knuth, who was accompanying them.

Krinsley recalls that historic first visit to the island:[5]

> "We flew then to Kaffeklubben Island, and we were there probably an hour and a half. We took some pebble count, took some specimens, and we looked at the place. Bill took quite a few notes. . .and we took a photograph toward (Cape) Morris Jesup, you could just maybe catch it. And then from there we flew to Constable Bay and Cape Morris Jesup."

When asked, "did you leave anything on the island?" Krinsley replied:

"Let me just say this, it is possible. The crew, because they really didn't have anything to do while we were walking all over the place and taking pebble counts, pictures and so on, may well have built a little cairn. When you look at the photos you will see there are no big stones."

The crew did in fact leave more than a cairn on the island. On July 6, 2003, (the same month and day as the 1960 visit) Peter Skafte, a member of The Euro-American Expedition, found a film canister on the ground near the cairn. In the canister were two weather-beaten sheets of paper.[6]

The first sheet contained a brief summary of the group's mission and the signatures of all the individuals involved in this historic first visit to Kaffeklubben Island:

```
                        6 July 1960

On this date two (US Army) H-34 Hel(icopters landed)
here, H-34C's 549 (        908        at        )
TREOG Ft. Eustis (                    )
Departed Frederick E. Hyde Fjord this (        )
stopped here for geological and archaeological studies enroute to Cape Morris
Jesup.
We wish you godspeed and good fortune.
James W. Sandridge, Lt. Col., CO, US Army
David H. Lindsey, CWO, W2, US Army
Mike V. Mayville, CWO, US Army
John W. Gallagla, SP/6 US Army
Daniel B. Krinsley
Wilmer E. Larsen, SP-4. US Army
SFC Gould
Wysir Morton, CWO USA
Michael J. Madden, CWO US Army
William E. Davies, (US Geolo)gical Survey
Eigil Knuth
```

The second sheet was apparently the whimsical work of one of the crew members:

```
Maylin Gougalla the phantom (Cairn)
builders strike again.
When better cairns are bu(ilt)
out of rocks and sheer boredom
Maylin Gogalla will build them
We specialize in all nativ(e)
material cairns for Bay
island      rds. No(w)
is complete      hout one
Please do (not) disturb this
artifact of the plastic
age purchased at the
Thule BX        April 19
Maylin
Gougalla
```

Krinsley believes that John Gallagla with a little time on his hands, sheer boredom, and a whimsical nature became "Maylin Gougalla."

63

10

Peary Land

R. E. Peary, J. P. Koch, Lauge Koch and Sledge Patrol
Sirius are the only ones that have traveled the earth's
most northerly coast in the proper way, dog sledge.

—*Mogens N. Gulbrandsen*[1]

In 1906 the Commission for Direction of the Geological and Geographical Investigation in Greenland recognized the geographical significance of Peary's exploration of northern Greenland by designating the area north of Independence Fjord as Peary Land. The name, now found on almost every map of Greenland, is undoubtedly the most notable geographic recognition accorded him.

Despite Gulbrandsen's comment to the contrary, most Peary Land exploration since 1921 has been facilitated by aircraft of one kind or another. Lauge Koch returned in 1938, and rather than traveling by dog sledge, this time he flew over the area. The previous year, a Russian expedition drifting on an ice flow off the northeast coast of Greenland had reported seeing land. This news, combined with an opportunity to further investigate the interior of Peary Land, resulted in the Danish government authorizing Lauge Koch to form an aerial expedition to investigate both areas. To accomplish the mission, a Dornier-Wal flying boat was flown to Kings Bay, Spitsbergen, for the purpose of investigating the area between Greenland and Spitsbergen and the interior of Peary Land.

The flying boat made two flights. The first flew over an area off the northeast coast of Greenland, which did not reveal any land. The second flight flew over the southern half of Peary Land and allowed Koch to fill in several blanks that remained on his maps from previous expeditions to the area. He noted, "As we approached Peary Land the mountains grew higher and higher, and more and more details were discovered, several of which I recognized from my journey in 1921. . . I was busily engaged in measuring and sketching the landscapes over which we flew—large fjord systems, occasional lakes, mountain ranges, and glaciers."[2] The flight did not take him directly over Kaffeklubben Island and Cape Morris Jesup, but it did give him a more complete picture of the geography of Peary Land.

In 1953, two Swiss geologists, Earhart Frankl and Fritz Muller, became the next visitors to Cape Morris Jesup.[3] As a part of Lauge Koch's Danish East Greenland Expedition in 1953, they reached the cape from the south, rather than approaching it along the coast. This area of Peary Land, now known as Johannes V. Jensen Land, is a large peninsula bounded on the north and east by the Arctic Ocean, on south by the Frederick E. Hyde Fjord and to the west by several smaller fjords. A wide mountain chain with glaciated valleys runs through the land, and it was this mountain chain that was of interest to the two geologists.

The two men were flown by seaplane to a small fjord on the south side of the peninsula, and from here they began a northward trek following a valley through the mountains. On August 6th they reached the northern coast about eleven miles west of Cape Morris Jesup, and immediately headed east. They reached the cape at 8:47 a.m., and immediately examined the cairn. In it they found a rusty tin containing the Danebrog left by Koch and a brass case containing Koch's full report from 1921. They made a copy of the report that was left in place of the original along with a short summary of their trip. They then assembled some geological and botanical data before starting their return trip at 12 noon.

In the early 1960s, the Sledge Patrol Sirius traveled north Peary Land for the first time. The patrol, a long-range reconnaissance and surveillance unit of the Danish Armed Forces, was created in 1950 to maintain Danish sovereignty in North and Northeast Greenland and to police the Northeast Greenland National Park. Six teams, each with two members and eleven dogs, go on sledge trips of 1600 km from November to June. During this period, the patrolling sledge teams operate mostly alone and away from established support bases.

In 1964, the patrol made its first visit to Peary Land. One of the teams traveled along the southern edge as far as the J. P. Koch Fjord and the northwest Greenland coast, while a second team traveled up the northeast coast to the Frederick E. Hyde Fjord. Then in May and June 1965, the patrol traveled west along the north coast of Greenland, the first traverse of the coast by dog sledge since the days of Peary and Koch. It did not attempt to reach Kaffeklubben Island, but did camp at Cape Morris Jesup.

Sledge Patrol teams attempted to reach Kaffeklubben Island in 1967, 1970 and 1971. These were unsuccessful as poor ice conditions, loose snow, lack of supplies or tired dogs and men thwarted their efforts. It was not until April 12, 1974 that a team was successful in reaching the island, and to mark the occasion, they built a small cairn on the northern end of the island. [4] This cairn, along with the 1960 American cairn, can still be found on the island.

In 1969, a British Joint Services Expedition went to north Peary Land. [5] In addition to providing experience for potential leaders of future expeditions, the aims of the group were to explore the area north of the Frederick E. Hyde Fjord and to make attempts at climbing a number of peaks in the area. In addition a scientific program of survey, geology, glaciology, natural history and meteorology was undertaken. The main scientific aim was to complete a survey traverse that circumnavigated the northern half of Peary Land.

The traverse covered a measured distance of two-hundred-ninety-five miles, but it was significant that the total distance as shown on the existing maps was only two-hundred-seventy miles. In addition, detail-mapping errors were found along the north coast west of Cape Morris Jesup. The expedition report made the following comment with regard to the survey results, "By comparing this with the results of Lillestrand's 1968 and 1969 work (see following chapter) it will eventually be possible to resolve the controversy centered on Cape Morris Jesup and its claim to the title the northernmost land on Earth."

11

Nord

*. . .measurements made during the Spring and Summer of 1969
. . .place Kaffeklubben Island a distance of 0.2 nautical miles
farthernorth than Cape Morris Jesup, and as such it becomes
the most northerly point of land discovered thus far.*

—R. L. Lillestrand, E. F. Roots, E. R. Niblett, J. R. Weber[1]

In the early part of 1968, David Humphreys and his Arctic Expedition flew to Ward Hunt Island off the north coast of Canada with the goal of reaching the North Pole over the winter ice. After several failed attempts to make any headway toward the pole, Humphreys decided to salvage something from his expedition by flying to Cape Morris Jesup and checking Peary's 1900 position determination. At this time the only "on the ground" position fix for the cape was the one made by Peary sixty-eight years earlier. The suggestion for making the flight to the cape was made by Robert Lillestrand who, along with Fred App at the Control Data Corporation back in Minnesota, was calculating position fixes for the expedition as Humphreys radioed his raw data back to Minneapolis.

Thus, on May 6, 1968, Humphreys landed at what he and his pilot, Weldy Phipps, believed to be Cape Morris Jesup. While there he made a series of theodolite observations, which were radioed back to Lillestrand and App for a determination of the cape's latitude and longitude. The latitude turned out to be consistent with that obtained by Peary in 1900 and with those shown on existing maps. The longitude, however, was grossly different: eighteen miles when compared with that given by Peary and up to twenty-five miles when compared with existing maps. Humphreys' position fix placed him well to the east of all the accepted locations for Cape Morris Jesup.

At the time Humphreys made the observations, he also saw what appeared to him to be either a small island or peninsula. All but its northern tip was covered by snow and ice, and it could have been either. He noted its position relative to his location as approximately one mile to the east and one mile to the north. Since he thought he was in the vicinity of Cape Morris Jesup, he assumed that the island/peninsula he was seeing was a part of the cape's topography, and that it was the northern extremity. The cape is not sharply defined, but rather it has a broad, rounded shape, and given the snow and ice covering the area at the time, Humphreys' confusion is understandable.

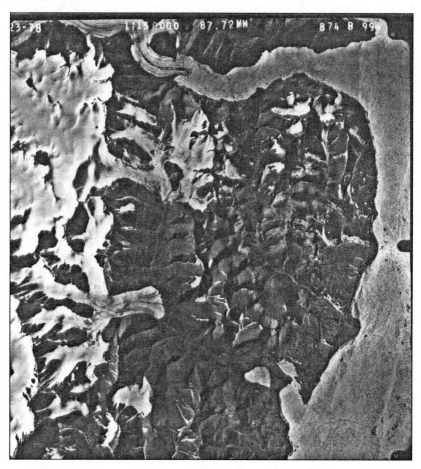

In an interview in *The New York Times,* Humphreys was quoted as saying "that the frozen, windswept Cape Morris Jesup on the northern coast of Greenland was actually twelve miles further east and a mile north of its position on all known maps."[2] Moreover he asserted the cape was an island, not a peninsula. In his mind, the idea was further validated by the fact that he had noticed a cairn on the island, which he assumed was the one built by Peary at Cape Morris Jesup in 1900.

App and Lillestrand wrote a report summarizing the results of the position fixes they had made for Humphreys.[3] Based on the data in their report, they came to the conclusion that Humphreys had been at Cape James Hill when the measurements were made, and that the island, which Humphreys had seen, was in fact Kaffeklubben. These were personal conclusions and were not included in their report. However, Humphreys' pilot continued to maintain that he had flown them to Cape Morris Jesup and not beyond it to Cape James Hill.

Given that Humphreys and Phipps could not precisely locate Cape Morris Jesup on their maps, it raised a question of map accuracy. Further analysis of existing maps of the area showed inconsistencies in the positions of many of these geographical features. The location of Cape Morris Jesup differed by as much as twenty-five miles between various maps. To investigate these suspected discrepancies, Lillestrand, Humphreys, and the author, sponsored by the Arctic Institute of North America (AINA), undertook Project Nord-1968 in August of that year. The staging site for Project Nord-68 was Thule Air Base on Greenland's west coast and the operational site was Station Nord, a Danish weather station in northeast Greenland.

During the planning stages, it was decided that both astronomic and satellite navigation techniques would be used to determine positions. The use of two different forms of navigation provided insurance against an operational failure by one or the other. The Transit Satellite Navigation System was originally developed for shipboard navigation and had been in use by the U.S. Navy since 1963. In 1967 it was released for nonmilitary use, and in the first half of 1968, receivers became commercially available. At that time the Bedford Institute in Dartmouth, Nova Scotia, received two units, and as a means of testing it in high latitudes, one unit was made available for use by the project[4]. Two theodolites, surveying instruments used for measuring horizontal and vertical angles, were used for solar astronomic observations.

Lillestrand, Humphreys, and Johnson were joined by David Wells from the Bedford Institute, Bruce Muscolino from the International Telephone and Telegraph Corporation in California, and Ralph Lenton from AINA. Project flights in Greenland were flown by Bradley Air Services, which provided a single-engine DeHavilland Otter aircraft piloted by John Jamieson. Also at Station Nord at this time were Count Eigil Knuth, the Danish archaeologist, and his assistant Oleg Andersen, who were there after a summer archaeological field season in northern Greenland.

Wells and Jamieson arrived at the weather station several days prior to the other project members and used the extra days to make a pair of preliminary reconnaissance flights. On August 28th, Jamieson flew Wells, Knuth, and Andersen over to Cape Eiler Rasmussen, where Wells set up the Transit receiver and left it in an unattended operative mode. The next day Jamieson flew the three back to Cape Eiler Rasmussen where they picked up the equipment and flew it to Cape Morris Jesup. This was the first airplane to land at the cape. Once there they set up the Transit receiver, but as a storm was moving on to the cape, there was not enough time to collect sufficient data before Jamison had to take off. Knuth and Andersen offered to stay behind and tend the equipment while also doing some exploring. Jamieson and Wells intended to return the next day, but weather delayed the return flight for five days.

On August 30th, the U.S. Air Force flew Lillestrand, Johnson, Humphreys and Muscolino from Thule to Nord. Conversations between Lillestrand, Johnson, and the plane's navigator before and during the flight were the beginning of a series of events that eventually lead to defining the world's most northerly point of land. Knowing that the goal of Project Nord was to investigate the accuracy of the maps of Peary Land, the navigator mentioned that on previous flights between Thule and Nord he noticed that the distance between identifiable points on his flight map often did not agree with the same distance as determined by the plane's ground speed. These discrepancies were not consistent and varied by their general location on the map. He noted, however, that they tended to be east-west, rather than north-south, i.e., errors of longitude rather than of latitude. They weren't large enough to cause him problems, but large enough to bother a serious navigator. These observations, along with the "questionable" results of the Humphreys' expedition earlier that year, led project members to request the pilot take a flight path that passed along the north coast of Greenland.

The weather was clear and the pilot agreed to reduce the plane's altitude from 7,000 feet to 2,800 for the purpose of observing and photographing the coastal area in the vicinity of Cape Morris Jesup and Kaffeklubben Island. Three passes over the Cape didn't reveal any surprises (at the time the presence of Knuth and Andersen was unknown, and the aircraft was still too high to note any human activity). After the third pass, the plane continued east along the coast with Kaffeklubben Island coming into view. The island was noted, mostly because of it historical significance, but Lillestrand commented that, "Kaffeklubben could be at least as far north as Cape Morris Jesup." Given the slight south-east direction of the coast, the altitude of the plane, and the distance between the two, there was no way to verify the idea from the air. At the time it just raised one more question concerning the relative accuracy of the maps. Another hour and the plane reached Nord, disembarked the team's four members and returned to Thule. Only then did they find out that they and flown right over Knuth and Andersen.

An attempted flight the next day, August 31st, to Cape Morris Jesup with all five project members on board had to be aborted about thirty miles from the cape because of possible icing, poor visibility, and blowing snow on the ground. The flight then diverted to Valdemar Glucksadt Land and to Cape Renaissance where conditions were satisfactory for landing and for astro-observations. Low clouds and blowing snow grounded the plane for the next two days at Nord. Prior to this, the beaches in the area had been clear of snow, and the pilot was able to land at the desired sites without great difficulty. After this many of the proposed landing areas became permanently snow covered and were no longer accessible. (It was still possible to land at Cape Morris Jesup because the pilot had the foresight to mark out a runway on the first flight there.) Although there were still 24 hours of daylight in the region, the pilot preferred not to fly during the hours near midnight because of the long shadows and marginal levels of light created by the low angle of the sun.

Late on September 3rd weather conditions improved and a flight back to Cape Morris Jesup was again possible. The additional weight on the return flight, two men and six-hundred pounds of electronic equipment, allowed space for only Lillestrand and Johnson to accompany the outbound flight. As the plane landed, using runway markers set out during the previous flight, clouds were slowly moving over the cape. By the time the theodolites were set up the sun had disappeared completely behind the clouds precluding any astronomic observations. The Transit generator had failed after only four satellite passes, but these proved sufficient to obtain the first latitude and longitude at the cape since Peary's 1900 fix. After several photographs and an inspection of the cairn built by Peary in 1900, the plane was loaded for the flight back to Nord.

The next day Jamieson flew the Otter to the Canadian base at Alert landing at Bronlund Fjord, Wandels Dal and Cape Wallen along the way. On board the flight were Lillestrand and Humphreys, who made a series of astro-observations at each of the sites. Also on board was Squadron Leader Frederick Scott of the Royal Air Force who inspected Bronlund Fjord as a possible landing site. He and a Royal Air Force C-130 had arrived at Nord the previous day to evaluate various sites for a British Joint Forces expedition to take place the following year in North Peary Land. That same day, Johnson, Wells, and Muscolino stayed at Nord to obtain a final set of astronomic and Transit observations, and the next day the RAF C-130 flew the rest of the team to Alert also. From there expedition members returned home either to the United States or Canada.

The results of Project Nord-1968 indicated map errors up to fifteen nautical miles, primarily in a longitudinal or east-west direction[5]. This led to the conclusion that northern Greenland was approximately 2,500 square nautical miles larger than heretofore shown. Historically there is a logical reason for these longitudinal errors. When making astronomical observations, an error in the observer's chronometer leads directly to an error in longitude, while this same timing error has only a minimal effect on the latitude. The early explorers were often in the Arctic for years with little or no opportunity to check their chronometers. They usually carried several chronometers and checked one against another in an attempt to reduce any accumulating errors, but during extended expeditions it was impossible to maintain accurate time. These errors led directly to longitudinal inaccuracies. This type of error diminished over the years as radio time signals became available, but many maps incorporated information obtained during the late 1800s and early 1900s. Until 1968, there had in fact been no position determination for Cape Morris Jesup since the one made by Peary in 1900.

In 1969, the U.S. Air Force Aeronautical Chart and Information Center published its new series of Operational Navigation Charts (ONC). ONC A-1 and A-5 superseded earlier World Aeronautical Charts (WAC) of the same area. Based on the work of Project Nord-1968, cautionary notes were added to the ONC charts for Northern Greenland.

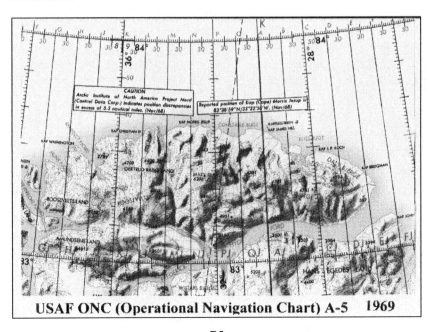

USAF ONC (Operational Navigation Chart) A-5   1969

The goal of Project Nord-1968 had been to investigate mapping errors across all of Peary Land, not to determine what might be its northern most point of land. However, while flying along the north coast of Greenland past Cape Morris Jesup and Kaffeklubben Island, the question had again arisen, "Could the island be farther north than the cape?" When this visual observation was combined with what Humphreys had seen earlier that year, the possibility became more compelling.

To answer the question and to establish additional ground control points to the west of Kaffeklubben Island, a follow-up project, Project Nord-69 was initiated. This was carried out as Phase II of the Canadian North Pole Expedition of 1969. On the morning of April 18, 1969, R. L. Lillestrand and E. F. Roots were flown in a Twin Otter aircraft from Station Alert on the northeast coast of Ellesmere Island eastward along the Greenland coast to Kaffeklubben Island. Along the way, they made a series of position determinations using an Omega airborne electronic positioning system. At Kaffeklubben Island, they landed on the sea ice next to the island and proceeded to take three hours of solar observations in order to determine a precise position. Although not the first persons to visit the island, they were the first to determine its latitude and longitude. After finishing their observations, they flew the 20 miles back to Cape Morris Jesup. They first spent several hours placing a fuel drum marker at the northern extremity of the cape and then took a series of solar latitude observations before returning to Alert.

From the latitudes obtained from these two sets of observations, taken under similar conditions and within several hours of each other, they determined that Kaffeklubben Island is 0.2 nautical miles farther north than Cape Morris Jesup[6] This established a new geographic location for the "northernmost point of land," and the island began to claim it rightful place on maps and in arctic history.

Part Three Ghost Islands

Ghost Islands, yes

—Leif Vanggaard[1]

12

Oodaaq Island

I drew my companions' attention to the item, and—although
still in doubt—I announced that I had discovered a new island.

—Uffe Petersen[1]

Since 1969, when it displaced Cape Morris Jesup, Kaffeklubben Island had been accepted as the northernmost land in the world. Then, in 1978, a small island, even farther to the north, was discovered. During that summer a joint operation involving the Danish Geodetic Institute and the Geological Survey of Greenland was undertaken in Peary Land. The purpose was to establish ground control points for a new orthophoto map of North Greenland and to obtain gravity measurements in the same area.

The mapping group was comprised of five geodesists divided into two teams, one of which included Uffe Petersen and Frede Madsen. The following recollection by Petersen is particularly noteworthy in that it is the first in a series of island discoveries that continue to this day:

> A special assignment this year was to settle the discussion, which had been going on for years, whether Cape Morris Jesup or Kaffeklubben Island was the northernmost point of the world. The latest observations stated that Kaffeklubben Island was a few hundred meters closer to the North Pole than Cape Morris Jesup.
>
> The first step for Frede Madsen and myself was to install the Doppler satellite instrument on Cape Morris Jesup. To collect sufficient data on the tape recorder, the instrument has to work for at least a few days. Meanwhile, we measured

by theodolite and tellurometer (an electronic instrument for distance measurement) to the outermost points at the shore of Cape Morris Jesup – and enjoyed life at our camp.

On the 26th of July we were picked up by the Heliswiss helicopter, which had started early in the morning from the base camp at Fastelavnsso in Jorgen Bronlund Fjord. The plan was to install the Doppler instrument on Kaffeklubben Island, carry out theodolite and tellurometer measurements to points on the northern shoreline of the island, and then – after a few hours work – return to our camp on Cape Morris Jesup, leaving the doppler instrument to collect satellite data during the next days.

Working from helicopters usually is very intensive. This day was no exception. After landing we immediately started programming the satellite predictions into the Doppler instrument, establishing the ground point, marking the point on an aerial photograph, and taking photographs of the surroundings, etc. The last task was to measure the shore points of the island with the theodolite. During the measuring work I had a small break and decided to have a look northward, hoping to find tracks from previous expeditions. Instead I saw a thin shadow on the sea ice almost due north. My first thought was that it was a black iceberg. From other regions of Greenland I knew that icebergs coming from the bottom of a glacier often are black due to mixture of soil from the ground. But since there are no active glaciers in this region, I immediately rejected this idea. After a closer study with binoculars and theodolite my next assumption was that the shadow consisted of gravel. I drew my companions' attention to the item, and – although still in doubt – I announced that I had discovered a new island, only to be met with laughs. However, I insisted, and after they had the opportunity to study the shadow, they did not reject my assumption and agreed that the item required further investigation.

It was decided that Frede Madsen should fly to the position, and if a landing was possible, he should identify the object, and we should measure the distance with the tellurometers (tellurometer measurements require manned instruments at both ends of the line).

Using the theodolite I saw the helicopter having difficulties finding a proper landing site on the fragile and soaked ice, but after a few minutes the pilot succeeded. A moment later I received an amazing message on the walkie-talkie, the shadow on the ice really was a new island. Frede Madsen established a geodetic station on the island, and we measured the distance between the two stations. I completed the determination of the position of the new island by measuring the azimuth angle to the Doppler station at Cape Morris Jesup.

Our tellurometer measurements immediately revealed that distance to the new island was 1.36 kilometers, well beyond the uncertainty of the previous position determinations of Cape Morris Jesup and Kaffeklubben Island. At that time we did not know the positions measured by the Doppler instrument, since this required comprehensive computer analysis, which could not be carried out in the field. However, we were certain that we had found a land point further north than any land point recently known to be the northernmost point of the world.

Then I was picked up by the helicopter, and after a tour of the island at low altitude, we went back to our tent on Cape Morris Jesup, and the helicopter returned to base camp. Next day we finished the theodolite measurements at the doppler station on Cape Morris Jesup by measuring the azimuth angle between the doppler station on Kaffekluben Island and the stations along the shoreline of Cape Morris Jesup.

Three days later the Doppler instrument on Kaffeklubben Island was picked up by the other geodetic team, Hauge Andersson and Anders Faerch Jensen. This group also visited the new island.

I proposed the island be named Oodaaq Island after Oodaaq, one of the outstanding Thule sledge drivers who brought Peary to the North Pole in 1909. This name became official in 1980.[1]

The following summer, in 1979, two geologists, Svend Funder and Christian Hjort from the Danish Geological Survey visited the area and, in addition, a Sirius Patrol team also visited the area. Both teams reached what they assumed to be Oodaaq Island. In light of later discoveries, there is a question as to whether it was actually Oodaaq or whether they may have inadvertently stumbled onto other islands.

13

The ATOW/Euro-American Islands

*Quite accidentally, the 1996 ATOW Expedition, in the search
for Oodaaq Island, had discovered a new island that was now
proclaimed as the new northernmost point of land on earth.*

—John Jancik[1]

For seventeen years following the 1979 expedition, there were no further attempts to reach Oodaaq Island or to verify its claim as the world's northernmost land. On many newly published maps, it appeared as just to the north of Kaffeklubben Island.

Then, in 1996, the American Top of The World Expedition[2] (ATOW) led by John Jancik and Ken Zerbst, arrived in northern Greenland with the twin objectives of reaching Oodaaq Island and of climbing some of the world's northernmost mountains. At this time Oodaaq Island was still considered to be the only island north of Kaffeklubben. After flying to Station Nord, a Danish weather station in northeast Greenland, the ten members of the expedition were flown in two separate groups to Bliss Bay on the north coast, nine miles east of Kaffeklubben Island.

On July 7th, prior to landing, the second group made a short reconnaissance flight north of Kaffeklubben Island. They spotted what they thought was Oodaaq Island, and had the pilots give them a GPS reading of the island's latitude and longitude. In addition they also took several photographs of the island, The island, which was observed again in 1998 by Peter Skafte and visited in 2003 by the Euro-American Expedition came to be known as the 2003 Euro-American Island.

On July 10, 1996, the ten expedition members set out to reach their goal by first walking the nine miles along the coast and then the mile and a half out to Kaffeklubben Island. They soon discovered that much of the crossing would have to be made by wading through melt water on the sea ice surface. Halfway out to Kaffeklubben, they decided they needed additional equipment and supplies and so returned back to shore. Five of the party members then made an 18-mile roundtrip back to their base camp at Bliss Bay to get snowshoes and additional food. After obtaining the supplies, the entire team set out once again for Kaffeklubben.

The snowshoes were a great help and, after more than two hours of wading in and out of meltwater, the team arrived at Kaffeklubben. Here they stopped for lunch, drained their boots and wrung out their socks. Oodaaq, which should have been about three-quarters of a mile north, was not immediately visible, but they spotted a dark spot on the ice, which seemed as if it might be the island. Breaking into smaller search parties they started out in the general direction of the spot guided by two members, with whom they were in radio contact, back on Kaffeklubben. When they reached it, however, all they found was a pile of dirty snow. They then broadened the search, but still were unable to find the island. The two team members on Kaffeklubben, Steve Gardiner and Jim Schaefer, then decided to join the search. They soon saw another "black spot," which "turned out to be a rock, two feet long and eight or nine inches wide, sticking three inches out of the water in the middle of a pool some 30 or 40 feet in diameter." They had come upon a small island, which they assumed was Oodaaq Island, but they took a set of GPS readings to precisely establish the island's location. After taking photographs of each of the members who had reached the island, the team returned to the mainland.

During the next two days, several members returned for quick visits. During each of these visits, the question arose as to whether the island they had reached was actually Oodaaq. The island's GPS position did not quite agree with the coordinates established back in 1978. (Non-military GPS receivers used during 1996 had their positions routinely degraded by the military for security purposes.) The

84

thought lingered, but since their coordinates seemed to be reasonably close and the later visits determined that the island although flooded was bigger than it first appeared, the thought of a new island was put aside. Having accomplished their first objective, the expedition then proceeded to climb several mountains in the previously unexplored H. H. Benedict Range.

In May 1997, *Life* magazine published a series of photographs taken by Galen Rowell during the 1996 ATOW Expedition. Several people at the Danish Polar Center (DPC) saw the photographs and began to question whether the ATOW Expedition had in fact visited Oodaaq Island. The photographs and the island's description did not agree with what they knew about the island. During the summer of 1997, the Danish National Survey and Cadastre (KMS), the former Danish Geodetic Institute, had a survey crew in Peary Land, and in July, Rene Forsberg and the KMS helicopter crew made a flight out to Kaffeklubben and beyond to evaluate the "island situation." They were unable to find either Oodaaq or the 1996 ATOW Island. What they found was yet another island on which they landed. This island, about fifty meters by fifty meters in size, was northeast of Kaffeklubben, but not as far north as Oodaaq or the 1996 Island. Thus a third or fourth new island (1997 KMS Island) was added to the map.

In the summer of 1998 Dennis Schmidt, a member of the 1996 ATOW Expedition, led his Euro-American Expedition to the north coast of Greenland.[4] Although this was primarily a climbing expedition, Schmidt made a reconnaissance flight over the area north of Kaffeklubben, and during this flight Peter Skafte noted two rock features north of the 1996 ATOW Island . He photographed them but was unable to get a precise position fix.

In the spring of 2001, 1996 ATOW Expedition members John Jancik, Terri Baker and Ken Zerbst reunited to form a second expedition to Peary Land, the Return to the Top of the World (RTOW) Expedition[5]. Prior to the expedition, research conducted by Jancik and Tony Higgins and Willy Wang of the Danish Department of Geological Mapping (GEUS) led them to the conclusion that neither the 1996 ATOW Island nor the island seen by Forsberg in May of 1997 (the

"1997 KMS Island") were in fact Oodaaq Island.

The appearance of these islands and the seeming disappearance of Oodaaq led individuals at the Geological Survey of Denmark and Greenland (GEUS) to re-evaluate the "northernmost island" claim and, in June 2001, Higgins e-mailed Jancik with the conclusion that the 1996 ATOW Island was "slightly further north than Oodaaq Island." This news reached the RTOW expedition members just as they were preparing to depart for northern Greenland.

The expedition's primary goal had been to climb several mountains in the Roosevelt Range, but given the new information, they also planned an aerial reconnaissance of the northern islands. On one of the early positioning flights, Hauge Andersson from the Danish Polar Center (DPC) joined the group as they flew over the northern islands. During this flight they were able to spot both the "1996" and "1997" islands, but found no trace of Oodaaq. More importantly, David Baker spotted two more islands even farther to the north. These were then photographed and their position obtained using the plane's GPS equipment.

After returning to the United States, individuals from the RTOW Expedition, KMS, GEUS and the DPC began evaluating all the island sightings. It was apparent that Oodaaq Island no longer existed and that at various times there had in fact been several islands north of Kaffeklubben. In October 2001, the Danish Polar Center posted on their Web site an article, written by Terri Baker and Hauge Anderson of the DPC, titled "New Islands, New Northernmost Point of Land on Earth Discovered off Northern Greenland's Coast." This was the first published announcement that Oodaaq Island had not been seen since 1978 and that other islands north of Kaffeklubben had been visited by foot or seen from the air.

Continuing his interest in the area, Dennis Schmitt led another Euro-American Expedition to the region in 2003.[6] This time, rather than just flying over the islands, Schmitt wanted to reach them by foot. After being flown to the coast, expedition members first walked out to Kaffeklubben and then continued north over the sea ice for about a mile looking for the small island that Skafte had first seen in 1998 and that the RTOW Expedition had seen in 2001. About two miles of north of Kaffeklubben, they came upon an island, approximately twenty meters long and four meters high, with vegetation that seemed to indicate that it had been there for several years. The team felt they were indeed standing at "Ultima Thule," the world's most northerly point of land, even as they realized that it, too, would probably disappear.

In May 2004, all of these smaller islands seemed to have disappeared. During that time Rene Forsberg of the Danish National Survey and Cadastre (KMS) had occasion to make several flights over the area, and his observations are summed up in the following e-mail exchange:[7]

John Jancik to Rene Forsberg: "In Willy's (Willy Weng, GEUS) e-mail he noted that you were unable to find/see/identify any of the small islands north of Kaffeklubben Island. Is this information correct? If so, what do you project as the reasons that none of these small islands were visible? (Perhaps a fresh snowfall might have covered them up)?"

Forsberg to Jancik: "We took quite a lot of passes over there on May 25 (2004). There was no new snowfall. I assume all "major" islands basically were scraped over by the ice... unlike May 2002 when one of the islands was clearly visible."

It was evident from Forsberg's flights and his report that these "ghostly apparitions" had disappeared once again. Then, in July 2007, Dennis Schmitt led another of his expeditions to Peary Land.[8] This time, he located and reached an island that had not previously been charted or visited. Not as far north as some of its predecessor islands, it was still a half-mile farther north than Kaffeklubben Island, but since Schmitt did not look for or fine any of these islands he may or may not have reached a new *ultima thule*.

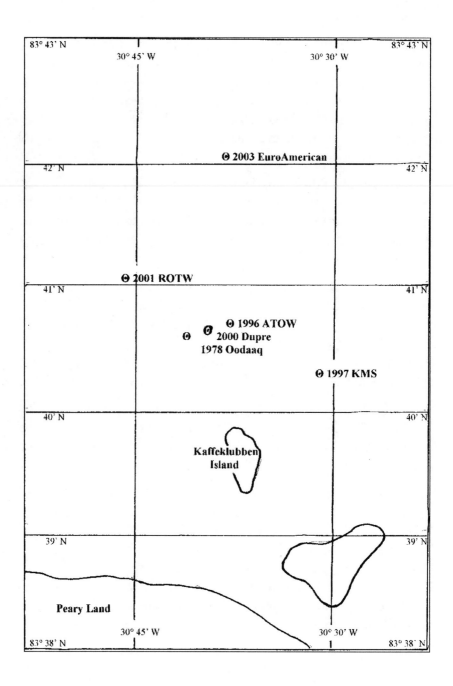

14

Epilogue

But surely there will be another summer
when someone will come looking.

—Peter Skafte[1]

The quest to reach the "highest," the "deepest," or the "remotest" points on earth has always drawn adventurous individuals. The *ultima thule* of ancient philosophers and the *ultima terra firma* of historical explorers is certainly one of earth's "remote" places, and for hundreds of years adventurous individuals have felt compelled to seek it out and to fix its location on arctic maps and charts.

Kaffeklubben Island currently holds the distinction as the world's "northernmost" piece of land, but what then of the ghost islands? Like an apparition, will they continue to appear and disappear, or could one of them someday become permanent and replace Kaffeklubben Island as a new *ultima thule*? Currently they appear, exist for a relatively short time, and then because of the varying formations of the ice, blowing snow and/or melting conditions they disappear. Future changes in the arctic climate could conceivably alter their transitory nature.

Thus, because there is a possibility of a new *ultima thule*, explorers and scientists will continue to search beyond Kaffeklubben Island for a dark spot on the ice. A new island will almost certainly appear again one of these years, ghosts always seem to come back to their old haunts, and just possibly, this will be the one that will be lifted out of what Peary called the "mists and obscurity" of northern Greenland to replace Kaffeklubben Island as a new *ultima thule.*

89

Appendice A & B

Chronology of the Geographic
Exploration of Peary Land

51-51   The First Grinnell Expedition sails to the Arctic in search of Sir John Franklin. The expedition's two ships, the *Advance* and the *Rescue*, are under the command of Edwin J. DeHaven. The expedition's surgeon is Elisha Kent Kane.

55-55   The Second Grinnell Expedition, under the command of Kane, sails to the Arctic. The expedition's ship *Advance* is locked in the ice and finally sinks forcing the crew into a hazardous retreat in open boats. The expedition's surgeon is Isaac Israel Hayes.

61-61   Hayes leads his own expedition to the Arctic aboard the *United States*. He avoids disaster, but accomplishes very little.

73-73   Charles Francis Hall and his ship the *Polaris* reach a farthest north before Hall dies a mysterious death. The ship is wrecked, and the crew drifts for six months before being rescued.

76-76   The British attempt to regain Polar supremacy by sending two ships, the *Alert* and the *Discovery*, under the command of George Nares through Smith Sound to the Arctic Ocean. The expedition maps the NE coast of Ellesmere Island and the NW coast of Greenland and reaches a new farthest north over the sea ice on the Arctic Ocean.

84-84   The Lady Franklin Bay Expedition, better known as the Greely Expedition, is the United States' contribution to the First International Polar Year. The expedition led by Adolphus Greely sends two members to a new farthest north along the Greenland coast.

1886   Robert Edwin Peary makes his first venture into the Arctic failing in a modest attempt to cross the Greenland icecap.

92-92   Peary returns to Greenland and sledges some 500 miles to Independence Bay. He mistakenly believes he had reached the northern extent of Greenland.

95-95   Peary again sledges to Independence Bay, but accomplishes little in the way of geographic discovery.

1896   Peary returns to Greenland in an attempt to retrieve a large meteorite. Ice prevents him from landing.

1897   Peary again returns to Greenland and successfully retrieves the meteorite.

2-02   In 1900 Peary sledges along the north coast of Greenland establishing its insularity and eliminating the possibility of traveling by land to the North Pole. Along the north coast he declares a cape, which he names after Morris Jesup, as being the northern most point of land in the world. From the cape he starts north toward the pole but quickly abandons the attempt. Twenty miles to the east he notes and maps a small island, but he does not visit or name it. In 1901 he travels north over the sea ice to establish a new farthest north.

6-06   Peary makes another failed attempt to reach the pole. He starts from Ellesmere Island this time but returns by way of the north Greenland coast. He reaches land 65 miles to the west of Cape Morris Jesup, and being short of supplies he foregoes any further exploration and heads immediately for his ship the *Roosevelt*.

1909   Peary claims to have reached the North Pole. As a back-up in case he drifts to the east on his return he sends two men, George Borup and Donald MacMillan, along the north coast of Greenland. They travel as far as Cape Morris Jesup where they make several tide observations before returning to the *Roosevelt*.

1921   Lauge Koch, the first Dane to do so, traverses the north Greenland coast. He stops at Cape Morris Jesup thinking it to be the northern most point of land. Twenty miles to the east he also notes the small island. He does not visit it, but does give it a name, Kaffeklubben Island.

1938   Flying from Kings Bay in Spitsbergen, Lauge Koch makes the first flight over Peary Land.

1953   Two Swiss scientists participating in the Danish East Greenland Expedition reach Cape Morris Jesup by traversing north from Friggs Fjord through the interior of Peary Land.

1960   An American team from the U. S. Geological Survey investigating possible aircraft landing sites in Peary Land fly by helicopter to both Kaffeklubben Island and Cape Morris Jesup. They are the first to set foot on the island and the first to fly to the cape.

1964   A Danish PBY (Catalina) aircraft lands on the lake in Constable Bay, and the Danish Sledge Patrol Sirius travels to Peary Land for the first time.

1965   The Sledge Patrol Sirius makes a west bound traverse along the north coast of Peary Land camping at Cape Morris Jesup.

1968   In May the Humphreys Arctic Expedition attempts to fly to Cape Morris Jesup, but unknowingly lands 13 miles to the east. The locations determined by their astronomical observations raise questions concerning the accuracy of existing maps. In late August an American Expedition, Project Nord, flies to Cape Morris Jesup and several other Peary Land sites for the purpose of investigating suspected map errors.

1969   A joint Canadian-US expedition, Project Nord 1969, flies to Kaffeklubben Island and Cape Morris Jesup. It determines that the island is farther north than the cape. The British Joint Services Expedition circumnavigates North Peary Land, starting and finishing at Cape Morris Jesup.

1974   The Sledge Patrol Sirius makes its first visit to Kaffeklubben Island.

1978   A Danish Geodetic Institute expedition to North Peary Land discovers a small island to the north of Kaffeklubben Island. It is named Oodaaq.

1979   Two Danish geologists and the Sledge Patrol Sirius make separate visits to Oodaaq. These are the last confirmed sightings of the island.

1996   The American Top Of The World (ATOW) Expedition reaches a new island north of Kaffeklubben Island and sees another island farther north.

1997   A Danish National Survey and Cadastre expedition revisits the area north of Kaffeklubben Island and discovers another island.

1998   During a flyover the EuroAmerican Expedition sights two possible islands north of Kaffeklubben Island.

2001   The Return To The Top Of The World (RTOW) Expedition returns to north Peary Land and sights their 1996 island and another possible island even farther north.

2003   The 2003 EuroAmerican Expedition returns to north Peary Land and reaches the two islands seen by them in 1998 and seen by the ATOW Expedition in 1996 and the RTOW Expedition in 2001.

2004   A KMS flight makes several passes over the area and finds no evidence of any of the islands.

2007   Dennis Schmitt leads another expedition to Peary Land. He finds a new bit of land half a mile north of Kaffeklubben Island.

Chronology of "Other" Expeditions to North Peary Land

1991   Peter Brandt's expedition reaches North Greenland.

1996   The Norwegian G2 Greenland Expedition (Rune Gjeldnes and Torry Larsen) reaches Cape Morris Jesup after a northward traverse across the icecap from Cape Farewell.

1999   John Andersen, kayaks around North Greenland.

2000   The International Greenland Expedition (Lonnie Duprey and John Hoelscher), as part of a circumnavigation of Greenland, traverses the north coast by dog sled.

Appendice C

North Peary Land Geographic Features

Feature	Lat/Long (Determined)	Date, Expedition (Sighted or Visited)
Cape Morris Jesup*		
	83° 38' 41" N 33° 20.5' W	1900, Robert Peary
	83° 38' 59" N 33° 22' 56" W	1968, Project Nord
	83° 39.8' N	1969, Project Nord
	83° 39' 38" N 33° 23' 37" W	1978, Danish Geodetic Institute

*Some coordinate variation is the result of where on the cape the observations were made and the translation, if any, to the perceived northernmost point.

Kaffeklubben Island		
	83 40.1' N 30° 37' W	1969, Project Nord
	83° 39' 54" N 30° 37' 45" W	1978, Danish Geodetic Institute
	83° 39' 48" N 30° 39' 12" W	2000, International Greenland Expedition
Oodaaq Island		
	83° 40' 33" N 30° 40'10" W	1978, Danish Geodetic Institute

"1996 ATOW" Island

83° 40' 35" N	1996, Top of the World
30° 38' 39" W	Expedition
	1997, Sirius Sledge Patrol (Aerial reconnaissance)
	2001, RTOW Expedition (Aerial reconnaissance)
	2002, KMS (Aerial reconnaissance)
	2003, Sirius Sledge Patrol
	2003, EuroAmerican Expedition

"1997 KMS" Island

83° 40' 15" N	1997, Danish KMS Expedition
30° 30' 35" W	(Aerial reconnaissance)
	2001, RTOW Expedition (Aerial reconnaissance)

"2000 Dupre" Island (likely 1996 ATOW)

83° 40' 15" N	2000, International Greenland
30° 30' 35" W	

"2001 RTOW" Island

83° 41' 06" N	2001, Top of the World
30° 45' 36" W	Expedition (Aerial reconnaissance)
83° 41' 05" N	2003, EuroAmerican
30° 45' 33" W	Expedition

"2003 EuroAmerican" Island

83° 42' 11" N	1996, Top of the World
30° 33' 14" W	Expedition (Aerial reconnaissance)
	1998, EuroAmerican Expedition (Aerial reconnaissance)
83° 42' 03" N	2003, EuroAmerican
30° 38' 30" W	Expedition

Bibliography

App, F.N. and R.L. Lillestrand. "Analysis of Measurements made by Humphreys Arctic Expedition when at Cape Morris Jesup, Greenland." Internal publication of the Control Data Corporation, Minneapolis, Minn., June 1968.

Brainard, D.L. *Six Came Back,* Indianapolis, Ind.: The Bobbs-Merrill Co., 1940.

Bridgeman, H.L. "Peary's Progress to the Pole." *Bulletin of the American Geographical Society,* Vol. XXXIII, 1901, pp. 425-431.

Davies, W.E., and D.B. Krinsley. "Evaluation of arctic ice-free sites Kronprins Christian Land and Peary Land, North Greenland 1960." Air Force Cambridge Research Laboratories, *Air Force Surveys in Geophysics,* No. 135, 1961.

Fränkl, E. "Across the Mountains of North Peary Land," *The Mountain World,* Swiss Foundation for Alpine Research, 1954, pp. 169-184.

Greely, A.W. *Report on the Proceedings of the United States Expedition to Lady Franklin Bay, Grinnell Land* (2 vol.) Washington: Government Printing Office, 1888.

Grønnow, B., and J.F. Jensen. "The Northernmost Ruins of the Globe." *Meddelelser Om Grønland · Man & Society,* Vol. 29, 2003.

Hayes, I.I. *The Open Polar Sea: A Narrative of a Voyage of Discovery Towards the North Pole, in the Schooner "United States."* New York: Hurd and Houghton, 1867.

Jancik, J., S. Gardner, and J. Richardson. *Under the Midnight Sun.* Greenwood Village, Col.: StarsEnd Creations, 2003.

Jancik, J.S. "The Far North." *The American Alpine Journal,* Vol. 46, 2004, pp. 250-251.

Kane, E.K. *Arctic Explorations: The Second Grinnell Expedition* (2 Vol.). Philadelphia: Childs and Peterson, 1858

Koch, L. "Report on the Danish Bicentenary Jubilee Expedition North of Greenland 1920-23," *Meddelelser Om Grønland,* Vol. LXX, 1927, pp. 1-232.

————. "Survey of North Greenland," *Meddelelser Om Grønland,* Vol. 130, 1940, pp. 1-364

Laursen, D. "The Place Names of North Greenland." *Meddelelser Om Grønland,* vol. 180, No. 2, 1972.

Lillestrand, R.L., and G.W. Johnson. "Cartography of North Greenland." *Surveying and Mapping,* XXXI, No. 2, 1971, pp. 233-250.

Lillestrand, R.L. and E.F. Roots, E.R. Niblett, and J.R. Weber. "Position of Kaffeklubben Island," *The Canadian Surveyor,* Vol. 24, No. 1, 1970, pp. 142-145.

Nares, G.S. *Narrative of a Voyage to the Polar Sea During 1875-6* (2 vol.) London: Samson Low, Marston, Searle & Rivington, 1878.

Peacock, J.D.C. *Joint Services Expedition North Peary Land 1969,* London: 1972.

Peary, R.E. *Northward Over the Great Ice* (2 vol.) New York: Stokes, 1898.

————. *Nearest the Pole.* New York: Doubleday, 1907.

————. *The North Pole.* New York: Stokes, 1910.

Richardson, J.H. "Journey to the End of the Earth," *Esquire*, October 2007.

Schledermann, P. "Notes on Norse Finds from the East Coast of Ellesmere Island, N.W.T." *Arctic*, 33: 1960.

Schmitt, D. "The Far North." *The American Alpine Journal,* Vol. 46, 2004.

Skafte, P. "Searching for Ultima Thule," *The Polar Times,* Vol. 3, No. 5, 2004; Vol. 3, No. 6, 2005; and Vol. 3, No. 7, 2005.

Tyson, G.E. *Arctic Experiences.* New York, Cooper Square Press, 2002.

Weems, J.E. *Peary the Explorer and the Man.* Boston, Houghton Mifflin Co. Press, 1967.

Wilford, J.N. "Northernmost Tip of the World Is Said to Be Mapped Incorrectly," *New York Times,* May 29, 1968.

Index

Notes